A MUSICAL MOTLEY

A
MUSICAL MOTLEY
By ERNEST NEWMAN

LONDON: JOHN LANE, THE BODLEY HEAD
NEW YORK: JOHN LANE COMPANY. MCMXIX

*Printed in Great Britain
by Turnbull & Spears, Edinburgh*

TO

VERA

PREFACE

THE following articles have all appeared in various newspapers and journals during the last few years. Here and there a trifling alteration has been made, or a date inserted to show that the article was written at a time when something that is now ancient history was either quite new or as yet unborn.

Some apology is perhaps due for the liberal mixture of articles that are, in intention at any rate, gay, with articles that many readers will no doubt find excessively grave. But there are many quarters-of-an-hour at concerts during which even the most hardened critic must succumb to an attack of insomnia. In these moments of suffering he must either go mad and deal death all round him or see himself and his sad profession humorously. I have always preferred to try the latter remedy.

E. N.

CONTENTS

Contents

A MUSICAL MOTLEY

A

A MUSICAL MOTLEY

" L'ENFANT PRODIGUE "

I AM one of those who can just dimly re-member having seen *L'Enfant Prodigue* in their early youth, but have hardly any memory of its details. When I saw it again the other day, therefore, it had all the interest of a new work for me. Some of my musical friends, I observe—Mr Baughan, for example—honestly confess to having been a little bored by it all. I am thankful to say I am not yet so *blasé* as that. I enjoyed it hugely; it is a very charm-ing entertainment that I hope to see many times more. For people who are a little tired of the ordinary theatre, the ordinary concert, and the ordinary opera, and cannot at present get the Russian ballet, this seems to me just the thing they want. To musicians especially it is a relief to get away for a time from the chanted word of opera and yet have the human interest, not only in the music but on the stage. This kind of musical-mimetic art stands midway between the opera and the symphonic poem: it improves on the latter by giving us visible beings with whom to sympathize, and on the former by removing that old source of irritation, the inability to hear the words, by the simple process of dispensing with words.

For my part I confess to a sneaking liking for M. Wormser's score. I was astonished, indeed, to find how vital the bulk of it still is, in its own simple, unassuming way. But the very success of this modest effort set me wondering why some composer of the first rank does not make a bolder experiment in the same *genre*. I am not belittling M. Wormser. He has done marvels, considering the meagre means he has chosen to adopt. The piano strikes one at first as a nuisance. There is no more horrible tonal combination in existence than that of a piano and the strings of an orchestra: only a generation still hardly more than half-emerged from musical barbarism could tolerate the combination as it does in the ordinary piano concerto. But as you get deeper into *L'Enfant Prodigue* you begin to realize that M. Wormser knows a thing or two that you have never known or in your impatience have forgotten. Apart from one or two things like the buzzing of the bluebottle in the 'cello—which, I am almost ashamed to let Mr Baughan know, I enjoyed like a schoolboy—the composer obtains all his realistic effects on the piano. That instrument has not, of course, anything like the pictorial resource of the orchestra, but it is incomparable in certain effects of humorous realism. Moreover, by bringing in the orchestra only for the more purely musical utterances, the composer heightens, by very contrast, the passional and pathetic force of these. The reward for his previous reticence is that each orchestral stroke now counts double what it would have done had the same instrumental colour been used all the time. But while admiring, as we are bound to do, the singular skill and judgment M. Wormser has shown in the handling of his meagre material, we cannot help wondering what the effect would be with a larger orchestra and a more ambitious emotional scheme than he has permitted himself. Effects almost incredible in the way of realism —the pointing of gesture, the suggestion or accompaniment of movement, and so on—can be made with the modern orchestra, as every student of Strauss and Stravinsky knows ; and of course on the purely expressive side M. Wormser does not explore one-twentieth of the depths of modern music. Imagine what any one of the greater living composers could do, for example, with the poignant entrance of the Prodigal Son in the third Act, which M. Wormser has treated, it seems to me, a little too thinly and cursorily even for the marionette scale on which he is working.

What chiefly interested me, apart from the excellence of the performance—especially that of Mr Ronald at the piano—was the hint the work gave of the possibility of as yet unimagined developments. This mimodrama is a distinct art-form. Nothing can take its place and do its work. Spoken drama lacks the emotional in-tensification of music. Opera gives the singers words to utter, but under conditions that make it almost impossible to hear them ; moreover, with everybody but a Chaliapine, the positions of the mouth necessitated by singing deprive the actor of nine-tenths of the ordinary opportunities to enlighten and move the audience by facial expression. The ballet gives us music and wordless action; but in the ballet the dance element must always predominate over the dramatic, and most ballets, truth to tell, are rather childish in their scenarios. The musical mimodrama *is* music and *is* drama. It can show us character in action even more fully and subtly than opera can do; yet it can make use of opera's tremendous orchestral expression. Would it not be possible, then, to enlarge the scope of the wordless musical play far beyond that of *L'Enfant Prodigue*? Some such idea as this seems to have been in Strauss's head when he planned *The Legend of Joseph*. But he foundered on two rocks—the stupidity of Count Kessler's ponderous Teutonic didacticism, and the timidity that still held on to the ballet as a necessary part of the dramatic scheme. But wretched as Strauss's music to that work mostly was, he gave us, in just one splendid page, a hint of what music can do in the way of heightening the effect of a silent stage scene—I mean the tense expectancy of the music to the episode in which Joseph slowly makes his way up to Potiphar's wife, who passes her necklet over his head. A long serious work written on the same expressive scale as that one page would be marvellously moving; and there seems no reason why it should not be done.

For many literary schemes, of course, the old operatic form cannot be dispensed with : we could not imagine *The Meistersingers*, for example, in any other than its present form. But the nearer an opera approaches pure emotion, the less words become necessary, the more capable is music of taking on its shoulders the whole burden of the emotional expression, simply calling in the gesture of the living actor to *préciser* the feeling from moment to moment. When one reflects on it, most of the literary bases of music amount to mere local dressings of the same eternal theme. Most symphonic poems and programme symphonies boil down to the contest between forces of good and evil— whether in the form of " Fate " as in the Fifth Symphony of Beethoven and the three last of Tchaikovski, or in the form of men and women as in the numerous Hamlets, Richard the Thirds, and so on. When the musician has to sing of love, neither words nor milieu matter very much. Paris and Helen, Aucassin and Nicolete, Paolo and Francesca, Romeo and Juliet—the emotions and the springs of emotion were the same in all these, and the time and the place are as much the merest trimmings as are their costumes. Shall we not arrive some day, by the sheer cancellation of one purely literary effort by another—all possible forms of literary expression being exhausted as the forms of sculpture are on the way to being—at the eternal symbols that lie at the base of all dramatic poetry ? The musician will not ask whether it is Helen or

Francesca, Macbeth or Napoleon, Grace Darling
or Casabianca, Till Eulenspiegel or Scapin.
He will simply say to himself "love," or
"ambition," or "devotion," or "roguery," and
strike straight to the heart of the symbol, un-
trammelled by considerations of latitude and
longitude, climate and costume. What has music
—the greatest music—to do with all these? A
work like *L'Enfant Prodigue,* small in scale as
it is, is enough to show us the potency, for
musical purposes, of character quintessentialized
into the type: for it is largely with the type,
rather than the individual, that music has to
deal. It was a stroke of genius on the part of
M. Carré and M. Wormser to show us the father
and the son in the symbolic form of Pierrot *père*
and Pierrot *fils.* Our first idea is that the expressive power of the characters is limited thereby; but we soon learn that it is really expanded.
Paradoxical as it may seem, the most expressive
faces on the stage are those of the father and
the son, with their background of dead chalk-
white. The reason is that these faces start, as
it were, from scratch, and every millimetre of
expression is seen as a real advance; whereas
the faces that remain as in real life begin at
nearly the top of their mimetic pace and energy,
and hardly any advance is possible. The Pierrot
begins with a cancellation of all the lines that
life has made in his face, which is thus a virgin
dead-white wall. Against this wall of all negation
the slightest movement of the eyes or the mouth
—the two most expressive features of the face—

stands out like a silhouette. Admirable as is the work of Yvonne Arnaud as Phrynette, Eugénie Nau as the mother, and Louis Gouget as the Baron, they are not only in another key than that of the two Pierrots, and a discrepant key, but also, from the point of view of expression, in a lower key. I imagine each of these characters would gain by being translated frankly into the symbolic, as Pierrot *père* and Pierrot *fils* are. Reality and the symbol do not blend. If it be asked whether we could bear Paolo and Francesca with whitened Pierrot faces, I would answer, tentatively, that in the right kind of setting, with the right actors and the right music, we should never think of them as Paolo and Francesca, any more than we think of M. Pierrot and his son as living in a certain town and having a couple of lines to themselves in the local directory. But I fancy we should be greatly moved as we lived again for an hour through all the tragic experiences of two of the world's great symbolic lovers.

A TRAP FOR CRITICS

ACCORDING to a report in the *Musical Times*, two fiendishly ingenious criminals in Manchester have invented a diabolical new musical game, designed, apparently, for the amusement of the public and the confusion of the critics. "Mr and Mrs Frank Merrick," we are told, "gave a recital of music for two pianofortes, when the works were not only unfamiliar, but the composers' names were withheld in order to give the music greater freedom to make its appeal, yet with no idea of mystifying the hearer." (Ahem!) "Of course one may derive added stimulus to pure enjoyment from endeavours to 'spot' the composers. A fortnight later there appeared in the advertisement columns of the *Manchester Guardian*, 'Hope Squire and Frank Merrick beg to announce that the three items presented at their recent concert were by Reger, Schubert, and Delius. The Reger duet has not previously been played in England.'" That is all: not a word of apology, not a hint of the fear that legislation may have to be invoked to prevent this infernal business going any further.

It is only in the critics' interest that I protest against it: for the public I think it would be a very good thing to have to listen to their music without knowing the title of the piece or the name of the composer. They would find the range of enjoyable music enormously multiplied for them. Most people at present are scared away by unfamiliar names. The plain man will not go to a concert if he sees the name of Brahms or Delius or Sibelius or Scriabine on the programme, because, not knowing anything about these composers, he is doubtful whether he will understand their music. If he would only try the experiment he would generally find that he understood it quite well and liked it very much. If he could be got to a concert by the bait of the Pathetic Symphony, or the " 1812 " Overture, or one of his other half-dozen standing dishes, and made to listen to a couple of unfamiliar works in total ignorance of their composers' names, he would listen more keenly and more honestly, and would be astonished afterwards to find how far he had travelled along roads that he thought were barred to him as one of the uninitiated. It is really much harder to listen honestly than one would imagine. There is generally an unconscious bias, for example, in favour of a work or a performance that comes from someone whose reputation for good things is well established; we see this in the applause that is showered upon the quite mediocre singing of some middle-aged prima donna. If the audience could hear her without knowing who she was, they would be much less impressed; but what they really hear at the concert is not the mere performance of the moment, but this plus all the reverberation of fame that has accompanied the lady for the last twenty-five years. Put her before an audience not hypnotized by familiarity with her record, and the chances are that they will see her more nearly for what she actually is. A few years ago an elderly prima donna who had fallen on evil days made a farewell tour. She had at that time no more than the merest remnants of what was once a fine voice ; but the ordinary concert-goer's physical pain at some of the sounds she produced was mitigated by a sympathetic memory of other days. But when she sang at the music halls the gods shrieked with laughter at the spectacle of a voiceless singer performing nonsensical Italian roulades. It was sad to see, but one could not blame them. It *was* a ridiculous exhibition to anyone who could take the performance just as it stood.

If we could all of us always see things in this detached way, as if we were newly arrived visitors from another planet, some of our artistic judgments would certainly be altered. Now and again we find ourselves put to the test. A few years ago somebody or other played as an encore a flute solo that I described in a notice next day as touching the very depths of inanity. A scandalized friend thereupon asked me if I knew that the piece was by Mozart. I did not ; and not knowing that, and therefore not being hypnotized by Mozart's name, as my friend had been, I could see the melody for the empty, perfunctory thing it was. It would be splendid, then, if we could have at least one experience of this kind at every concert we went to ; the pursuit of art would become a new and delightful form of adventure. But this, as I have said, while well enough from the point of view of the public, or of the critic *quâ* member of the public, is not to be thought of from the point of view of the critic *quâ* critic. Those great and good men have trials enough to bear already, without being called upon to decide publicly who wrote a given piece of music and what is the intrinsic value of it. It may be objected that they are always pronouncing at large upon the value of this music and that. Yes ; but we have the composer's name to help us, and that makes all the difference. Let it be remembered what unreasonable things are expected of us already. A pianist is not expected to know anything but a few pianoforte pieces, or a singer more than a few songs. But a critic is expected to know all the songs, piano music, violin music, organ music, 'cello music, orchestral music, operas, and oratorios ever written. Even under the present system of telling him the composer's name he makes a bad blunder now and then. A very good English critic once heard César Franck's violin and piano sonata at a concert, and wrote excellently about it. A week or two later he heard Franck's 'cello and piano sonata, and wrote equally excellently about that, though he appraised it quite differently from the violin sonata. There would have been no harm in this but for the fact that the two sonatas are one, the violin part being simply transposed for the 'cello compass. My friend did not know this, and "gave himself away" shockingly to people who did. But this is what we should all be doing if the Merrick plan of concert-giving were adopted everywhere. I for one should be in a fog on an uncharted sea, without a compass. At present a few simple rules are enough to guide my innocent practice. I have a rough idea, that is, what to think of a piece of music if I am told whether it is a symphony or an opera, and whether it is by Beethoven or Bach or Wagner or one of the other well-known fellows. But to have to sit all through a concert and not know whether it is fugues or symphonies or scherzos or tangos you are listening to, or who on earth wrote the baffling stuff, is enough to drive any critic mad. And to find next day that you had sniffed at a Bach *Passion* in the belief that it was a little thing of Coleridge Taylor's, or patted Brahms on the back for being the composer of some laborious thing by Ebenezer Prout! Even in the other arts, where the work more or less tells its own story, it is sometimes hard enough to make out what it means. A picture of La Karsavina by one Kauffmann was recently exhibited in Liverpool. The French admirers of that charming dancer were horrified to find her described by a local critic as "a crumbling ruin, a devastated gorge, a leprous façade, cracking and peeling—a dreadful vision, giving an unforgettable impression of tragic horror." The mystery was solved only when it was discovered that the French packer had sent in error a wild landscape to the exhibition, to which the committee had attached the title of the picture they understood the artist to be sending them. How was an art critic in Liverpool to know that *La Karsavina* was not a landscape but a Russian dancer? And Mr George Moore has recently told us how puzzled he and his friends once were over a certain sonnet by Mr W. B. Yeats. "Even the adepts could not discover whether it referred to a woman, a city, or a sailing-ship. A. E. inclined to the opinion that it was on the House of Lords; and the poet, being written to from Ely Place, replied that the subject of his sonnet was Coole Park." But in painting there is at least the subject to guide a critic, and in poetry, though the words may be obscure, still there *are* words; and in any case the critic of painting or of poetry can go back to the puzzle as often as he likes. But there is no going back in the concert room or the opera house, and neither the subject nor the language is always clear without some clue. What could any critic make of *Elektra* for example, played on the Merrick plan? He might just catch a word or two of it here and there, and on the strength of that describe it as a melodrama about Mad Maggie the Malevolent Mill Girl. Scriabine's *Prometheus* he might take for "A Windy Day on Hampstead Heath," or the *Symphonia Domestica* for "A Crowded Hour in the Life of a Munition Worker." If Mr Merrick finds many imitators we shall have a critics' strike before long.

ANALOGIES

SOMEBODY, either in the Bible or Shake-speare, once expressed a desire that his enemy would write a book—obviously in the malignant hope and belief that the enemy, not being quite at home in literary expression, would be unable to open his mouth without putting his foot in it. An old friend of mine, Mr Cyril Scott, has recently written a book— no less than a book of poems; and I find Cyril Scott the poet throwing such a flood of light on Cyril Scott the musician that I cannot help wishing that all the musical friends whose psychology I am trying to get to the bottom of would open a similar window for me into their souls. Not, of course, that I should long have the privilege of calling them friends after that; for if nothing pleases a critic more than to find another man out, nothing annoys the other man so much as the consciousness that he has given himself away. But after all, the critic is more at home in enmity than in friendship. The latter is a variable quantity; about the former there is a satisfying finality. No man whose horrible business it is to criticize others can be sure of how long he will keep a friend; but an enemy, he knows, is a permanent acquisition. To the critic a friend is merely a delicate annual, while an enemy is a hardy perennial; and while the critic cannot get any man's friendship by merely asking for it, the number of the enemies he can acquire depends entirely on himself.

I wish, then, that all my musical friends would write books so informative as this of Mr Cyril Scott's; if they would, I myself should be prepared to milnerize the consequences to our friendship. For here Mr Scott has given himself up naked to his critics. The defects of his poetry are so unmistakably those of his later music that anyone who may have been in doubt as to the latter can doubt them now no longer. When Mr Scott writes this, for example ;—

> In that upon the horologe of life the destined number
> Had reached that digit of fate's crescent, which unbends
> The cords of nescience and allows the lustre
> Of spirit-bliss to pierce its vesting rinds;

or this—

> We few, so love-entwined, and beauteously blended,
> Entethered to the dulcitude of our sublimed ideal,
> Garnered a saintly glimpse of the divinely Real,

he commits just the same fallacy in verse that he sometimes commits in his music—he mistakenly imagines that a vision not clearly seen by him in the first place can be imposed upon the reader, in spite of its obscurity and its lack of outline, by means of resonant and parti-coloured diction. For anyone with the soul of poetry in him recognizes at a glance that Mr Scott himself has never really seen the thing he is vainly trying to make us see in these lines of his; if he *had* seen it, it would limn itself for

B

him almost without a conscious effort on his part, and limn itself clearly, simply, and directly. So with his later music; he only needs to employ those self-conscious and self-willed exoticisms of harmony and rhythm because he is not sufficiently master of his idea to be able to see it clearly and express it directly. There is in logic a "law of parsimony" that forbids us to look for a remote explanation when one that sufficiently explains the facts lies near to our hand. There is a similar law of parsimony always unconsciously operating in the really great creative artist; he instinctively goes straight to his point, and then by the directest route from point to point; and the greater he is the less he fiddles and fumbles with his idea or divagates from it. What guides him is a sort of divine common sense. If we examine any great work of art, it is found to be as full of common-sense parsimony as a superb machine or a brilliant piece of scientific argumentation. Nothing in it is half-done or twice done; it is just done once for all. It is the smaller men who are always either half-saying what they want to say, or saying it twice or thrice when once would do.

Now in poetry or prose it is easy enough to distinguish an idea from its trappings; but in music it is much more difficult, because of the more complete fusion of the idea and the medium. We may have a vague feeling that a composer is not saying quite what he wanted to say, or not saying it with perfect lucidity; but we cannot completely segregate, as we can with all verbal expressions, the thing said from the manner of saying it. It is only when a musician expresses himself with approximately the same ease in another medium that we can be quite sure we understand the why and wherefore of his weaknesses. Beethoven's letters throw absolutely no light on his musical mind, because prose was not a medium in which he could think at all. But there are some composers the musical parts of whose minds are really illuminated for us by their work in other fields. The confusion of the later Schönberg is less incomprehensible to us after we have seen some of his paintings. Berlioz's prose illustrates his music in a remarkable manner. So it is, again, with Liszt, and to a smaller extent with Wagner. And if all composers were compelled by law, in the interests of psychology, to write at least one book every three years, we should find their literature throwing, as a rule, as much light on their music as we have seen to be the case with Mr Scott.

The whole man thinks, as George Henry Lewes said ; so it is not surprising that the personality of the artist should reveal itself in ways he never suspects. What is not generally recognized, however, is that people's instinctive dislike for this or that music is often due to their unconsciously formulating for themselves analogies between it and other modes of expression. They will dislike a shop ballad, for instance, because, unknown to them, it creates in them the same emotional nausea as a servant girl's novelette. In criticism it is desirable to cultivate this habit of seeing music in terms of prose or poetry or the other arts. The analogies are often closer than one would suspect at first, and nothing brings them out more saliently than parody. If I had wanted to parody Mr Scott's music at its worst, I should have tried to write poetry like this he has recently given us—though I should have despaired of achieving a parody of such deadly accuracy. If anyone wishes to clear up his ideas as to what is wrong with music that is obviously not right, he might do worse than try, for his own amusement, to translate its defects or absurdities into speech. He might take a nursery rhyme, for example— say "Baa, baa, black sheep"—and write a series of prose variations on it in the style of different composers. The gentlemen who are mad on harmony, and think they have added something precious to the world's wisdom when all they have done is to trick out a commonplace in gaudy vestments, would say "Baa, baa, black sheep" in twenty lines of polysyllabic neologisms and circumlocutions. These people are like the pompous simpletons who cannot call a barber a barber—he must be a "tonsorial artist"; people to whom an oyster is not an oyster, but a "succulent bivalve." Composers like Scriabine, who elect to work on a scale from which they have eliminated certain notes, resemble the man who should rewrite the nursery rhyme with an obstinate avoidance, say, of the

letters "e" and "s." The folk-music cranks
would rewrite it in archaic English. In the
blood-and-lust style of *Elektra* it would begin
with an oath and end with an obscenity. In the
style of the later Schönberg it would look as if
the compositor had dropped the type of the little
poem and put it together again in the order of
its picking up. In the style of Debussy it
would be full of mincing Parisian affectations.
In the pseudo-Oriental style the sheep would be
pulled up with a " Bismillah," and adjured in
the name of the Prophet to say how many bags
of wool he had, and how many sequins he would
sell them for. A poet of the Celtic twilight
would encourage the sheep with the information
that the wool was Deirdre's weaving. And so
on and so on. And when once anyone has
seen a musical absurdity in terms of an
equivalent absurdity of speech or line, he is the
less likely to be duped in the same way again.

"TRAUM DURCH DIE DÄMMERUNG"

EVEN at the time I had a suspicion that it was all a dream. It seemed too good to be true.

I remember being at a concert at which the pianist was putting himself to a tremendous amount of trouble to play the Tausig arrangement of Bach's D minor Toccata and Fugue, and not succeeding in playing it a quarter as well as the piano-player could do. I was wondering to myself at the strange blindness of some musicians to the march of events under their very noses. There are some pieces that no pianist can ever hope to perform as well as the piano-player: there are others that no piano-player at present imaginable can hope to perform as well as the best human pianist; yet it never seems to occur to public performers that they ought to keep to the latter and avoid the former. I suppose I must have been a bit bored by the performance, for I made no effort to resist the sleepy feeling that was stealing over me; and in another minute or so I was in a world in which the best performance of music has no power to charm, and the worst no power to hurt.

Suddenly I found myself in another and very different concert room—an enormous place, full of people, and with excellent music, excellently

the needed loudness by the extra number of instruments. This plan was scientifically sound enough, but it had the disadvantage of being expensive. The public still made a fuss of pianists in those days, and concert committees therefore had to pay them large fees. It seems curious that it should have been so, but the fact can be proved from historical documents. Well, the makers set themselves to overcome the difficulty by incorporating half a dozen piano-players in one, with the apparatus so arranged that the tone could be turned on with any degree of total or sectional power at the will of the operator. In a very little time the superiority of this instrument for concerto playing, and, indeed, for piano playing in general in large buildings, became so evident to all but the incurably prejudiced and old-fashioned that it was in universal demand for concert purposes, and the individual human pianist began to find his occupation going."

"But," I said, "I also heard singers and an orchestra at the concert. Were those also mechanical?"

"Yes," he replied—"mechanical, of course, in the best sense, not in the contemptuous sense in which, I believe, the word used to be applied to musical performances. After the gramophone— another primitive instrument of which we have some account in our libraries—it was a comparatively easy matter to invent a machine that could do everything the old-style prima donna used to do, and more. At first the manufacturers wisely avoided attempting to make the machine sing words.   They confined themselves to the production of vowel sounds, as the prima donna did.   A few purists, who wanted to make themselves disagreeable, raised an outcry in the press: they insisted that the words were as necessary in vocal music as the tone.   The makers made these people look very foolish by an ingenious device.   They invited a number of the noisiest of them to a conference, and having got them safely in a locked room, submitted them to a compulsory examination with a view to discovering how much they really knew or understood of the words of the music they most admired and heard most often.   It turned out that ninety-five per cent. of them knew no more of the words of one of the most popular prima donna arias, ' Caro nome,'—than simply—' Caro nome ': one per cent. of them could get as far as ' che il mio cor,' and only a half of one per cent. knew that this was followed by ' festi primo palpitar.'   In another test piece—' Una voce,' by an old composer named Rossini—it was found that only two per cent. of the purists knew that the rest of the line was ' poco fa,' and none of them had the faintest idea as to what came after that.   Nor could a single one of them give the examiners a rational account of what these and other arias were all about.   The results of the enquiry were published, and the stupid opposition was drowned in ridicule.

" The next thing was to give a competitive demonstration of human singers and mechanical

singers, like the one the piano-player manufacturers had arranged. The poor humans were,
of course, beaten off the field. They had neither
the power, nor the range, nor the accuracy, nor
the perfect intonation of the machine. By gearing
the mechanism up high, as it were, the aria could
be made to sound as if it were being sung at an
almost impossible height. I need not enlarge
on this : you can see for yourself how inevitably
and hopelessly beaten the prime donne were.
Then, after a hundred years or so of experiment,
the secret of producing perfect consonants was
discovered, and it became possible to produce
as faultless Lieder or operatic singing on the
machine as it was to produce faultless piano-
playing.

"So, to cut a long story short, it was with
orchestral instruments. The mechanically-played
violin and flute and so forth were easily made ;
then the problem was to subject them to thorough
artistic control. This problem was solved at last,
however, as it had been solved in the case of the
piano. Then the orchestra was concentrated and
simplified. A resonator attached to each instrument increased or diminished the tone of it _ad
libitum._ One violin could in this way be made
to do the work of five, or ten, or fifty. The next
step was to unite the governing principles of the
mechanism of all the instruments in one apparatus.
I shall have pleasure in showing you this one
day, for I am the manipulator of it at the concert-
hall we have just left, and, indeed, a member
of the International Syndicate that runs the

concerts.   The apparatus resembles the stops of
the old-time organ.   The music is cut for the
orchestra in just the same way as for the piano-
player.   All I have to do is to supply the more
delicate of the nuances.   I think I may take it,
Sir, that you were pleased with the results this
evening?"

I admitted that I was.

"Yes," he went on, "it has been a great
evolution, and the makers had sometimes to
exercise considerable ingenuity in order to overcome the prejudice of the public against mechanical music.   The greatest step, perhaps, was the
invention of the Predisposers, followed by that
of the Suggestors."

"What are these?" I asked.

"Oh," he said, "we don't use Predisposers at
all now, and the Suggestors very little; they
were only of assistance in the days when prejudice had to be overcome by a side rather than
a frontal attack.   Acute observers had noticed
that a particular pianist's or violinist's popularity
was due not so much to anything unique in his
playing as to something unique in his personality, or his appearance, or his circumstances, or
his history.   With one man it was his hair, with
another his eyes, with another his divorces, and
so on.   There were certain people called press
agents, whose business it was to create this
atmosphere about their clients—an atmosphere
that predisposed the public to see rather more in
these ladies and gentlemen than there actually
was.   So the makers of these playing and sing-

ing instruments at first had to *invent* human players for them—of course all the performances were given in the dark—and engage a number of people to predispose the public to believe about these quite fictitious performers everything that it was desirable that they should believe. These persons came to be known in the profession as Predisposers. They acted very well for a time. Then one manufacturer, more ingenious than the rest, said to himself, 'What really acts upon the public and makes it predisposed to see or hear what we want them to see or hear must be an invisible, impalpable mental force of some sort, communicated telepathically by the brain of the Predisposer to the brain of the Predisposed. Now why cannot we isolate this fluid, concentrate it, store it, and put it into operation just when and where we want to?' So he set his scientists experimenting, and in a few years they succeeded in isolating this force—which, indeed, had long been known to our stupid ancestors under the name of 'the force of suggestion,' though they were ignorant of its efficacy and of how to apply it—and a supply of it was laid on in the concert-room, where it is administered to the audience in small or large doses, without their being in the least aware of it, by a single operator who studies their faces from behind the curtain, and regulates the current according to the necessity for stimulating their enthusiasm. We call him the Suggestor, and mostly make use of him on the occasion of a performance of a new work. It is a profession calling for considerable knowledge of human nature and a gift for thought-reading —to say nothing of the mere management of the machine. We had a curious accident here a little while ago. The Suggestor, I grieve to say, partook too freely of alcoholic refreshment before the concert; and in a moment of abstraction he reversed the current. We nearly had a riot in the hall : many people came and demanded their money back. We calmed them down, however, by turning on an extra strong current of suggestion in the right direction.

"Well," said my companion, "here we are at the station. My train goes in a couple of minutes, so I am afraid I must leave you. I hope I have made it all tolerably clear to you?"

"You have," I said, "and I am greatly indebted to you. Just one question before you go. Did not all these changes impoverish the pianists and the rest of them? What became of them all?"

"Well," he said, "there was inevitably a little misery at first, but a paternal Government did all it could to alleviate it. The pianists and the vocalists were the worst off. For a time the Government gave the more able-bodied of them employment in making last ditches."

"Last ditches?" I said.

"Yes, last ditches for politicians to die in. It turned out, however, that the voluntary mortality among politicians fell short of the estimate, so the pianists and the others were glad to be drafted into a new profession—the teaching of people to appreciate and understand music. They taught the Art of Listening, and a jolly good thing some of them make out of it. It is curious that none of them ever thought of it before on their own account. Well, I really must run. Good-night." And he was off.

I woke up to find the poor devil on the platform making a feeble attempt to imitate, on the piano, the organ effects in the final bars of the fugue. It was lamentable, but the applause was terrific. Then I knew that the ancestors of the Predisposers and the Suggestors had been at work, and I took off my hat to these great men —the real artists of the musical world of to-day.

c

THE AMATEUR COMPOSER

I HAVE so often had the misfortune to sit on the opposite side of the house to Mr Francis Toye that it is a pleasure for me to be able to sit with him for once on the same benches. In the *English Review* he makes out a very good case for what he calls the amateur composer—that is to say, not the composer who writes like an amateur (none of us has any use for *him!*) but the composer who writes *as* an amateur, earning his living by some more or less honest business method, and practising composition more as a relaxation than as a profession. I think, with Mr Toye, that many a composer would do better work under these conditions; but I venture to disagree with him in his condemnation of the pot-boiler. If the artist is to go into business for a living, I do not see why he should not include among possible lucrative businesses that of writing pot-boilers— under an assumed name, however. It is surely no more of a sin to make money by turning out bad songs than to make it by turning out bad boots or razors or sausages. A certain amount of fraud is inseparable from business; and I see no reason why we should commend a Wagner, say, for earning the leisure and the comfort to write a *Tristan* by speculating in sugar—or even in young married women—and blame another composer for winning leisure and

34

comfort by speculating in that sentimental species
of British ballad that is to the emotions what
sugar is to the tongue. The only drawback to
this course, it seems to me, is that it is generally
much harder to sell a pot-boiler than to sell a
masterpiece. In the very nature of things, few
masterpieces can be written in any given generation; yet they all see the light at some time
or other. On the other hand, anyone can write
a pot-boiler; thousands must be written every
day; yet how many of them are ever published
or performed? Any fairly intelligent housemaid could write as bad a novel as Mr Charles
This, or Mrs Florence That, or the Baroness
the Other; but the luck of publishing and sales
would go only to one housemaid of them in a
thousand. But if the composer likes to try his
luck, I see no more moral objection to his
making money by swindling the public that
buys crotchets and quavers than there is to
his swindling the public that buys potatoes or
stocks and shares. None of us can live except
either by preying on someone else or by profiting
by the predatoriness of our fathers. But, as I
have hinted, while I should be unwilling to say
a word that would discourage the amateur
composer from making a good living by any
form of artistic dishonesty that came easily to
him, I should not recommend him to add
candour to his other failings. If he writes
pot-boilers, let him publish them under another
name; it would be advisable, in fact, for him
to choose for them a name that would skilfully

suggest that they came from the secret work-shop of a rival composer.

Practising composition purely as a hobby, a composer with anything in him would be tempted neither to over-write himself nor to appear before the public with a quantity of second or third-rate work from the mere necessity of keeping in the public eye or being forgotten. The sentimentalist will say something, no doubt, about the need for the artist having any amount of leisure so that he may be sure to be at home in case inspiration takes it into her head to call on him at any odd time. But to argue thus is to forget, as Mr Toye rightly says, that not one composer in a hundred actually lives under these conditions. Not one in a hundred has an independent income or can make a competency by first-rate work alone.

The bulk of them have to work as hard, and, from the point of view of "inspiration," as irrelevantly at music as they would have to do, under Mr Toye's scheme, at stock-broking or making hair curlers. They have to teach, or to govern conservatoires, or to conduct operas and concerts, or —the last degradation—to become musical critics. In any case they must have their mind on something else than composition for the greater part of each day, and must often come to their composition more fatigued and irritated than they would be after a day's good honest swindling in the rubber market, followed by a round of golf with a fellow criminal. If the great composer were more of a man, and less of a child who thinks the whole world ought to spoil him, he would see that all of his work that is worth doing could be done equally well in the leisure that business would give him, and perhaps with a cleaner and clearer mind. Hugo Wolf, in all probability, never really earned his own living for six months in his whole life; had it not been for the generosity of his friends he would have starved. Yet Wolf's total work amounts to no more than what a very busy man of business could have accomplished in his evenings, to say nothing of his week-ends and holidays. Wolf, too, was an extremely rapid worker; sometimes he would dash off a couple of songs in a night. Who can doubt that a day in an office would have done him less harm, both as man and as artist, than a day spent in the surroundings that ultimately brought him to his ruin, or in brooding angrily over his real or imaginary grievances, or in approaching, and being rebuffed by, concert conductors and operatic impresarios? People like this would surely be all the better for being compelled to earn their living in the ordinary way. If anyone is to be subsidized, I venture the humble suggestion that it should be not the writer of music but the writer upon music. The former needs for his creations nothing more than the stuff of his own inner consciousness; the latter needs time and money for endless and very expensive research and study, and the world gets much less than his best out of him because he has to earn, by five hours of uncongenial and irrelevant labour, the leisure for one hour of fruitful thinking. If any rich reader of these sentences, impressed by their logic and touched by their pathos, should wish to endow a writer upon music in order to set him free of the daily round for higher purposes, I shall try not to let false modesty stand in the way of giving him, in confidence, the name of such a one— one who, in consideration of a handsome endowment, would bind himself legally to work very hard, and not to spend more of each day on evil living than was absolutely necessary to keep his temperament in flower.

Mr Toye seems a little doubtful as to one or two effects that his prescription might have upon his amateur composer. Would it be good or bad for him to spend most of his hours away from the company of music and musicians? I should think it probable, on the whole, that it would be for his good. The trouble with most composers is that they know too much of other composers' music, or are too deferential to the ideals of their own day and circle. Stravinsky and Debussy, to name only these two, have shown us the value of the originality that consists in writing as if you had dropped on the earth from another planet, ignorant of what had been going on for so long on this, and looking at the world with the frankness of an impressionable child. The faculty for looking at things in one's own way is bound to be diminished to some extent by a wide familiarity with, and regard for, other people's ways of

looking at them. Given an artistic nature as
original as Stravinsky's, it would be an interesting experiment to deprive it from the beginning
of all knowledge of the classics. I should say
that a composer who really had something in
him would profit considerably by spending his
days and most of his nights away from professional musical chatter. And I cannot share
Mr Toye's fears that, whatever good his prescription might do the amateur composer in some
respects, it might make him technically somewhat less skilled than the composer who spent
all his time among music and musicians. The
composer who has the real thing in him will
always, with a very little training, make a
technique that will be quite adequate for his
ideas. Bach was mainly self-taught; so was
Elgar. Delius' technique has come from Delius,
not from his Leipzig teachers. Wagner and
Wolf, two supreme technicians, had practically
no professional teaching. On the other hand,
Glinka, as I have said elsewhere, died an
amateur because he was born an amateur; no
amount of training could have made a great
technician of him, for the simple reason that
no amount of training could have given him
the force or profundity or vivacity of thinking
that would have generated its own inevitable
technique. Borodin was an example of a composer with a large stock of enchanting original
ideas, but at the same time a born amateur—
though an amateur of the best kind. I think
he would have been just as much an amateur

at composition had he taken up composition professionally instead of chemistry. This amateurishness of technique does not show so much in his operas, for there it is helped out by the non-musical factors of the work. But it certainly shows in his symphonic and chamber music. Yet after all, an amateur like Borodin is worth fifty professionals like Saint-Saëns. There must be an immense amount of talent of that kind about, that would really be spoilt by the ordinary academic training,—talent that makes up for a certain lack of professional skill by the freshness of its ideas. And talent of this kind would be more likely to find its right expression by being cultivated for its own sake, as Borodin cultivated his, than by being sucked into the ordinary professional whirlpool.

ORIGINALITY AND THE AMATEUR

THE question of the amateur composer, raised by Mr Toye in the *English Review*, is perhaps worth still further discussion. Given a composer of real genius who, for whatever reason, was in the fortunate position of being able to practise his art purely as an amateur—I assume him, of course, to be a competent technician—would he be likely to find his originality helped or hindered by his amateurism? I do not forget that many of the composers of the past and of the present have had an independent income that has permitted them to write only what and when they pleased. But that is not quite what I mean by the amateur now. I have in my mind not so much a composer who is free of the necessity of writing music for a living as a composer who, after getting his technical training, has next to nothing to do with the professional world of music, and cares nothing about making his musical education complete by regularly attending concerts and listening to every sort of music from Bach to Bantock. "Amateur" is a clumsy term for such a man; but as no other single word can be found to describe him, "amateur" will have to do. The reader will readily understand the type I have in mind.

Before we can attempt to answer the question whether such a composer might be made more or less original by his circumstances, we must try to decide what originality means.   At the present day it is too often taken to mean a sharp departure from every other composer's idiom and line of thinking.   Thus Ornstein and Rebikov are in some quarters regarded as original composers, while a man like d'Indy is supposed to be one of the crowd.   But I think d'Indy could write something as strange and as good as *Les Rêves* or *The Wild Men's Dance* much more easily than Rebikov or Ornstein could write anything so good, without being at all strange, as d'Indy's pianoforte sonata in E minor.   It may be said, again, that *Hänsel and Gretel* is written in a traditional idiom, and any one of Erik Satie's fantasies in an original idiom ; but all the same we should most of us prefer an evening at the piano with Humperdinck to one with Satie, and there can be little question which of the two composers will be remembered and which forgotten fifty years hence.   It becomes evident already that there is an originality that matters and an originality that does not ; Satie's is an instance of the latter and Debussy's of the former ; while there is a type of mind that, without being original in the Debussy sense, also produces music that matters very much.   Wagner, for instance, sets us thinking of Weber and Beethoven, while Debussy sets us thinking of nobody in particular but himself ; but few would deny that Wagner is the greater man.   In the

Debussy sense, again, Bach is hardly an original at all; he merely did what all his predecessors and contemporaries did, but happened to do it very much better. The Rebikovs and Ornsteins and Pratellas and Schönbergs think of a number of things that never occurred to Bach, and that probably would not have occurred to him had he been of our own day; but all the same Bach "gets there," and the others do not. It was Chateaubriand, I think, who said that plenty of Napoleon's generals understood the art of war as well as, or better than, he did, but Napoleon had the knack of winning victories. Satie understands a lot about music that Grieg did not; but Grieg had the knack of winning musical victories. And after all, that is rather a useful knack, in art as in war.

It need hardly be said that no composer was ever held in respect after his own day unless he did something that no other composer did before or since. In this sense it is justifiable to speak of the originality not only of a Bizet but of a Gounod, not only of a Scriabine but of a Rachmaninov. All the composers whose names and works really live must have been original to some degree or other, yet ninety-nine per cent. of them have achieved their originality mainly within the range of the current idiom of their day. They may have expanded that idiom, or modified it here and there, but in the main they have spoken the common tongue, just as all our poets speak the same English, though they all manage to talk differently in it. We can isolate the characteristics of style that make *Pelleas and Melisande* what it is, but not the characteristics of style that make *Carmen* or Liszt's *Mephisto* waltz what it is; yet the originality of these two is as indubitable as that of *Pelleas*. It may be a different sort of originality; but that is another matter. Or, to take a more extreme instance, look at *Deh vieni alla finestra* and *Keep the home fires burning*. Each song uses the same simple diatonic idiom; Mozart has no more tones and colours at his disposal than the composer of one of the masterpieces of commonplace of our time; yet what a difference in the result! Here the secret of the originality is utterly undiscoverable, any more than the secret of the charm of a beautiful eye is discoverable; it is not a matter of cornea and iris, of rods and cones, for every eye has those; it is a matter of something within that we are all enraptured by when we see it, but that no analysis can explain. Within the ordinary language of music, again, an effect of originality may be made by some very simple turn that is given to melody or harmony. (I mean a durable effect of originality, not merely one that surprises us to-day and finds us wondering next week how we could ever have been surprised at it.) Every reader will be able to recall effects of this kind in poetry and great prose. Music is full of them. Analysis would show, I think, that Rimsky-Korsakov is peculiarly rich in this sort of effect. I could cite several examples from his songs; but one that everyone will be able to test for himself is the progression of four chords that opens the *Ivan the Terrible* overture and is occasionally employed in the opera itself. From the first three chords we confidently anticipate the fourth—and find ourselves completely wrong; yet—and this is the test of originality—however well we know the passage, the fourth chord always falls upon the ear with a touch of unexpectedness, just as no amount of familiarity with *The Tiger* can diminish the strange assaulting force of the "fearful" in

> "What immortal hand or eye
> Could frame thy fearful symmetry?"

Each time it strikes, it opens a new window in the imagination.

There are, then, three main varieties of originality, of which the one I have just illustrated—the giving of a subtle turn of unexpectedness to the common language—may be said to occupy the middle place. At the one extreme is the unanalysable originality of a Bach or a Mozart, who uses ordinary words, as it were, in the ordinary way, and yet makes extraordinarily imaginative effects with them. At the other extreme is the originality of the Stravinsky type, that makes a quite new language of its own for the utterance of quite new things. It is this last type that we may expect to see in greater profusion in the future, given the right conditions; and I imagine that one of the conditions will be the bringing up of composers of genius in as complete ignorance as possible of the work of the classics, ancient and modern. Some acquaintance with these is necessary, for an artist can no more afford to reject the fertilizing force of a great mind in his own genre than to reject the fertilising force of nature. But the contact ought not to go beyond what is necessary for fertilization; and everyone knows that the average composer has so much of other men's music pumped into him when he is young as to run the risk of having his own individuality swamped. The conditions, it will be seen, are changing. In the past, the great man generally came, like Bach or Beethoven or Wagner, as the climax of a tradition. But even in the past, and still more in the present, there is a type of mind whose originality comes from its being largely ignorant of, or insensitive to, the essence of other men's greatness. A Chopin, for instance, though necessarily acquainted with the music of his great predecessors and contemporaries, writes as if none of them had ever existed; and we may be sure that his music would have been substantially the same had he never heard of Bach and Beethoven. Berlioz, to whom criticism has not yet done justice, had a touch of the same path-breaking quality in him. There is more of it in Debussy and Stravinsky, and—though in a smaller degree than in those two—in Ravel. It is becoming clearer every day that music has the power, almost unsuspected before the present generation, of translating into tone the more impalpable qualities of visible nature. The older method of "painting" was by way of suggesting the externals of things—the undulation of the waves, the pealing of the thunder, and so on. The newer method is by way of suggesting the secret life that breathes in the things of nature. In *Jardins sous la pluie*, for instance, there is no formal painting, but there are marvellous hints of greenery, of coolness, of the gentle swish of rain, and of the smile of the earth and the flowers after a shower. *L'isle joyeuse* has no place on the map; it is any happy isle where the sunlight sends its golden shafts beating upon earth and wave. As in the impressionist picture, the chief character here is the light. No one can say what new territories in this direction music may still be able to conquer. With the subtilizing of civilization, the nerves become capable of seizing a thousand impressions from nature of which our forefathers knew nothing; and for many of these impressions music will have to find a voice. But it will be easier, perhaps, for a man of genius to develop his peculiar sensitiveness, and find the right expression for it, in proportion as he limits the clamour of other men's ideas within his brain. No composer of to-day can steep himself day after day in the great music of the past and present without his own individuality suffering. If he is perpetually engaged in teaching or conducting, his own powers of original thinking are bound to be to some extent dimished. And that is why I should be inclined to hope for more from an amateur of genius than from a composer who started out with the same native endowment, but was forced, for a living's sake, to immerse himself every day in Bach and Mozart and Beethoven and Wagner and Strauss. The finer strands in him would suffer as they do in the imaginative writer, poet or prosaist, who has to keep himself by busy journalism.

THE SMALL POEM IN MUSIC—I

MUSIC has so many advantages over the other arts that it can afford to be magnanimous and admit that it is at a disadvantage in two respects. In the first place, it has no beauty as a ruin. This, I suppose, comes from the fact that it exists in time, not in space, and that the ear cannot complete in imagination a broken record as the eye can. From what remains of the Parthenon or the avenue of Sphinxes we can, without much difficulty and with considerable accuracy, mentally reconstruct the original whole. It is, in the main, only a matter of supplying the missing repeats in a pattern. In music, however, though the pattern exists, the force of the repeats resides in the fact that they are not literal, but informed with ever new meanings by means of slight variations of melody, harmony or rhythm. When we say that music is sounding architecture we have to remember that it is an architecture in which pillars and arches and buttresses are not invariable but protean factors. Sculpture, again, in the state of partial ruin, has a great advantage over fragmentary music. The thesis might almost be maintained that statues like the Praxiteles Hermes or the Venus of Milos gain more than they have lost by being broken. The artistic imagination in us completes the missing curves, and even, perhaps, gives them

D

an ideal beauty that they may not have had in the original; while the sub-conscious emotion of pathos over the broken beautiful thing has probably something to do with our love for it. But music that is incomplete, either through the damage of the ages or through the composer's failure to finish it, is doomed. What imagination among us, given the first couple of pages of the *Tristan* prelude, could supply the third? Who could reconstruct the final pages of the first movement of the *Eroica* symphony from the themes of the earlier pages, as we can reconstruct the Parthenon from what remains of it, or as we can suggest two or three possible solutions of the problem set us by the missing arms of the Venus? So certain is it that music not completed by the composer has no chance of being completed, I will not say by the imagination of the casual hearer, as in the parallel case of statuary, but by the imagination even of the composer of ability, that it is the rarest thing in the world for the unfinished work of a composer to be published posthumously. Now and then, as with the Russians, a musician may add something to a dead colleague's almost finished opera; but as a rule the incomplete musical work is left untouched and unpublished. We have, in Hugo Wolf's last opera, *Manuel Venegas*, the case of a dead composer's uncompleted manuscript being published as he left it: and I know nothing more pathetic than this fragment. It ends abruptly in a casual bar with an unresolved discord; and so helpless are we in the face of unfinished music that, so far from our imagination being able to surmise the remainder of the scene, it is incompetent to give, for the mere resolution of this one discord, a suggestion so plausible that any half-dozen musicians would accept it as being the probable truth.

The second disability under which music labours is that apparently—though we cannot say what may happen in the future—it cannot be mightily expressive except on a fairly large scale. There have been some tremendous things said in a poetic quatrain, and some seminal things in a distich; but music requires space to deploy itself in before it can strike with overpowering strength. This is simply another aspect of the truth that a piece of music exists as a whole or not at all; since the whole pattern has to be revealed if the music is to tell its story, the smaller patterns are necessarily at a disadvantage as regards cumulative effect. And of course we cannot "quote" from music as we can from poetry. We can roll over our tongue a typical felicity, perhaps extending to no more than a line or two, from a long poem; but we can hardly sit at the piano and regale ourselves with a bar or two, or a modulation or two, from a symphony, as we can with such a line as

"The multitudinous seas incarnadine."

The only person I have ever heard of who could be quite happy with these musical pilules is Miss Skinner in *The Way of all Flesh*. The reader will remember that when Ernest

Pontifex remarked that he didn't much like Beethoven, Miss Skinner burst into a horrified protest: "Ah! how can you say so? You cannot understand him; you never could say this if you understood him. For me a simple chord of Beethoven is enough. This is happiness." No wonder Ernest was reminded of how her father had condescended to relax from his game of chess to take a little bodily nutriment; "Stay —I may presently take a glass of cold water— and a small piece of bread and butter"—which meant, in actual fact, some oyster patties, minced veal, apple tart, bread, cheese, and gin hot. Ernest inwardly translated Miss Skinner's remark into a sort of epitaph in Skinnerese:

> "Stay:
> I may presently take
> A simple chord of Beethoven
> Or a small semiquaver
> From one of Mendelssohn's Songs without Words." ·

Miss Skinner was to be envied: the rest of us would give something to be able to find complete happiness in a simple chord of Beethoven—to say nothing of a complex chord of Scriabine or Schönberg. It would open up a very wide field of enjoyment if we could savour by itself the wonderful bar in music as we savour the wonderful line in poetry. Most long musical works are too long, and the trouble is that it is very difficult to cut them. It is hard enough to do so in opera without leaving the rent in a deplorably unstitched state; while in instrumental music it is almost impossible. It is rarely that a smaller working version can be made of a symphony—Schubert's in C major is one of the few cases in which it can be done. In the more modern styles, such as that of Wagner, it is extremely difficult to condense the music even when the tissue of it is obviously made up, here and there, of excessive sequential repetitions; to cut a few bars out would not only destroy the rhetorical movement of the phrases but would land us in trouble with the key-sequences. It is a pity that it should be so, for it would be very agreeable if we could distil just the quintessence of an over-long work and take it in small doses. Craik found it both desirable and possible to bring out *The Faerie Queene* in an edition in which all the merely pedestrian stanzas were replaced by short summaries in prose. It is equally desirable, but quite impossible, to apply an equivalent method to Bruckner's symphonies, which are so rich in expressive detail but so sprawling, so inorganic as a whole. The day has evidently not yet come for a volume of music on the " Elegant Extracts " plan that used to delight those of our grandmothers who had a mild taste for poetry. We could piece together a most interesting scrapbook of this kind, containing, for instance, such things as the crescendo in the *Tristan* prelude, the " Death-devoted head, death-devoted heart," bars from the opera, the *Carmen* leit-motive, one or two wonderful modulations from Mozart, the tremendous chromatic passage for the orchestra and voices in Verdi's *Requiem*, the final bars of the *Crucifixus* in the B minor Mass, the cadences of the first theme of the slow movement in Grieg's pianoforte concerto; but the result would be like a museum that contained, under glass cases, the heart of St Francis, the hair of Helen, the nose of Cleopatra, and the biceps of Milo of Croton, from which we were expected to reconstruct the strength and beauty of a vanished world.

It being impossible, then, to isolate the felicities of music as we can isolate the felicities of poetry, our appetite for the small but pregnant musical expression can be satisfied only by works that correspond in size to the quatrain or the sonnet, but that are organic and complete. Is such a form possible in music?

THE SMALL POEM IN MUSIC—II

WHAT is the shortest complete musical work that has ever been written? So far as I know, it is one of Theodor Streicher's four settings of the *Sprüche und Gedichte* of Richard Dehmel. As so often happens, the very new thing has been done for the first time by a composer not of the first class. This little opus of Streicher's consists of four songs—if we can call them songs : perhaps aphorisms in music would be a better title for them. The fourth is of average length ; but the first runs only to eight bars, the third to nine bars, and the second to no more than four bars— which last I take to be the record in musical brevity. One or two of the little pieces are not wholly unsuccessful, though we always have the feeling that it was hardly worth while setting so much apparatus to work to say so little : it suggests a man taking half-an-hour to get a string of his violin in tune and then publicly playing a semiquaver on it : for few as the notes are in the smallest of these works, the *Leitspruch*, they seem rather many for the impression that is finally left on us. The collection as a whole does not destroy our belief in the possibility of musical song reduced to a nutshell ; it only makes us wish that some man of genius would try his hand at the genre.

But what I had in my mind when I began

these articles was not the small song but the small poem in instrumental music. My ideal is a piece of music of anything from ten (or even fewer, if practicable) to not more than twenty or twenty-five bars (thirty at the outside), that shall be complete, formally perfect, expressive, and, above all, shall give the impression that it has come from a quasi-poetic mood in the composer. Chopin gave us the model of the thing in some of his Preludes; and Scriabine— the modern composer who has done most in this field—gives the same title to the great majority of his shorter piano pieces, some of which conform to the ideal I have just sketched. What I am driving at is not simply the small piano work, however beautiful. Nothing of Scarlatti's, for instance, or any other of the older clavecinists, answers to my requirements. Indeed, no music before Chopin can possibly answer to them; for it was only with the Romantic movement that there came the real possibility of making a piece of purely instru- mental music the carrier of a poetic idea. None of the older programme music—not even the Lament in Bach's *Capriccio on the De- parture of a Brother*—comes within the scope of my definition, if only for the fact that the informing literary idea is stated by the composer in his title. Nor do even the quasi-poetical little pieces of Schumann meet the case: his *Réplique, Aveu, Coquette, Chiarina* and the rest of them are either musical pictures of real people, or else merely charming piano fragments to which the composer has attached a fanciful description. Mendelssohn's *Songs without Words*, of course, are ruled out. It is a song without words that I am asking for, but I am insistent as to the song. In the poetic sense, Mendelssohn's pieces are purely musical pieces : he has simply sat down to manipulate melodies and harmonies into pleasing shapes, for pure music's sake. What I want, and what we get in the few ideal pieces of the new genre that I shall shortly mention, is something over and above the music—not a poetic idea to which the composer or ourselves could give any literary expression, but all the same something that convinces us that when he took his pen in hand it was not simply as a musician but as a poet-musician, desirous of capturing a momentary mood which, if it flowers in music, has grown in a soil that we can only describe vaguely as poetry.

Chopin, as I have said, threw out the first hint for the new genre in his Preludes. But not all of them—indeed, less than half a dozen of them—answer to the ideal I have in mind. Many of them are barred by the fact that they are simply *music*, falling agreeably on the ear, but suggesting no mood on the composer's part beyond one of delight in making a beautiful pattern. Others are obviously " studies " in this or that aspect of piano technique. The really poetic ones are the second, the fourth, the sixth, the ninth, and the twentieth. The twenty-first almost comes within the scope of my definition, but it is a shade too long. The famous fifteenth is, of course, very poetic; but apart from its length, it is disqualified by the fact that its poetry is of the musical rather than the verbal order, so to speak: this prelude is really a sort of nocturne. But in each of the five that I have selected we feel, however incompetent we may be to express it in words, the impulse of a special sort of poetic feeling. The notes do not merely make beautiful patterns; we have the idea that something is going on at the back of the notes, as in, say, the C minor symphony. (I do not mean, of course, to imply any similarity of mood in the two cases.) How rare and presumably difficult a thing it is to seize one of these quasi-poetic moods and fix it infallibly in music is seen when we examine Scriabine's eighty or ninety Preludes and little pieces of the same order with a different title. Hardly a quarter of them are in the vein I have in mind. I should disqualify, for instance, both the first and the last Preludes of op. 8, lovely as they are. On the other hand, I should admit No. 1 of op. 27 by reason of its poetry, though, as it runs to thirty-five bars, it is rather too long. The ideal thing is something not only poetic but aphoristic: as I have said, even thirty bars are too many. It is true that the mere counting of bars is not always reliable, for a simple change in the method of notation might halve or double the number of these. The exquisite No. 5 of op. 11 has only fifteen bars, but it is written in 4/2 time; the piece might have been as logically written in common time, thus doubling the number of the bars. Perhaps a better way of defining the ideal length for this sort of piece would be to say that it should not exceed an ordinary page of music. None of Scriabine's best works in the genre go beyond this, while some of them, such as the fourth of op. 31, occupy only half a page. My list would be made up something as follows:—op. 2, No. 2; op. 27, No. 2; op. 22, No. 2; op. 17, No. 4; op. 15, No. 5; op. 11, Nos. 5, 10, 13, 15, 17, and 22; op. 16, No. 4; op. 48, No. 2; op. 39, Nos. 2, 3 and 4; op. 37, Nos. 1 and 3; op. 33, No. 1; op. 31, No. 4; op. 56, No. 3; op. 51, No. 2. No doubt students of Scriabine would put forward a claim for at least a dozen others. I do not think, however, that I have rejected these without reason. Some, for all their beauty, are what I have called piano pieces pure and simple. In others—and this is particularly true of the later works—the mood is one of fantasy rather than poetry— the two *Poèmes* for example, of op. 65, the *Masque* of op. 63 (No. 1), the *Caresse dansée* of op. 57; others, like the lovely op. 67, No. 1, have more of the quality of the *paysage*. Practically all of the twenty-two that I have selected are undeniably poetic, and have something of what I can only call the aphoristic about them. They obey a poetic rather than a simply musical *ordonnance;* they plunge into the very heart of their subject without preamble; they often end with a kind of query or an

aposiopesis, and they have throughout the air
of having set out to say something very definite,
which they say in the fewest possible notes,
every one of which plays a vital part in the
story; and having said what it set out to say,
the poem ends without rhetoric, without trimmings, without flourishes, without any of music's
usual attempt to make an effective exit from
the stage. That is the new genre—a most
beautiful and seminal one—that I have in mind.
Scriabine is the greatest master of it at present.
Will it be made to cover yet other portions of
the musical *terrain* by some future pianoforte
composer?

COMPOSERS AND OBITUARY NOTICES

THE war has pleasurably disappointed the expectations of many of us. At the commencement we imagined that the mortality among musicians would be so enormous that we would be kept busy writing obituary notices as long as the war lasted. After four years' slaughter, things remain much as they would have been in normal times so far as music is concerned, though of course there must have been a great loss of potential ability among the young men in each nation. The musical mortality list of the last four years has been more than usually interesting—(I speak now, needless to say, from the purely professional point of view)—but few of the names in it are there in consequence of the war. Among these few are those of Denis Browne, a promising young London critic, Reginald Stuart Welch, another young musician of great keenness and promise, Albéric Magnard, the French composer — who was shot by the Germans in their first advance for the crime of defending his own house—Jules Ecorcheville, one of the leading French writers upon music, who was killed in action in 1915 at the age of forty-two, George Butterworth, a young composer of much promise, and Granados, who was on the torpedoed "Sussex." A son of Safonoff was killed in service with the Russian Army, but I do not know whether he was a musician. Virtually all the remainder of the musical people of note who have died during the past two years have done so peaceably in their beds, away from war and war's alarms. Scriabine perished as the result of a scratched pimple; Max Reger died of an old heart trouble. Each of these men was of military age, but neither was serving. Debussy died of a long-standing malady. The remaining obituary includes Leschetizky, W. J. Samuell (the excellent young baritone), John F. Runciman, Natalia Macfarren, Frederick Jameson (the translator of Wagner), Walter van Noorden (head of the Carl Rosa Company), Stanley Hawley, C. A. Barry, Goldmark, G. W. L. Marshall-Hall, Sgambati, Stavenhagen, Taneiev, and Boïto.

In common with other journalists, I have a grievance against the ordinary musician. Death comes to all men sooner or later; but no man of eminence who is living quietly and safely at home, and can more or less choose the time of his own dying, has a right to depart this life without remembering his obligations of honour to his biographers. I speak feelingly on this subject, for some of these gentlemen have put me to a good deal of inconvenience by their irregular and inconsiderate way of dying. Many of those who still survive are very decent fellows, and I feel I have only to make my grievance known for them to recognize the necessity for a little kindly forethought on their part. The reader is aware, I suppose, that every newspaper office has its pigeon-holes crammed with obituary notices of people who are still living. There is nothing cynical about this—nothing so cynical as the notice a friend of mine once received, ordering him to serve the following Tuesday on a coroner's jury that was to hold an inquest on a man alive at the moment, but who was to be hanged at eight o'clock on Tuesday morning. The newspaper wishes its subjects no harm : it merely wants to be prepared for all contingencies ; and as there is no guarantee from a politician or a poet that he will have the decency to die in good time in the morning, and so give the journalist a whole day in which to prepare his obituary notice for the next issue of the paper, the only thing is to have the notice ready well in advance. In the last few years I have spent a great deal of time in the writing of obituary notices of musicians. It is rather difficult work, but work I like, especially when the subjects are my personal friends ; I find it very interesting to try to put myself—as the obituary writer should do—at the point of view of ten or twenty years hence, and see the man's whole work as if he had already been dead that length of time. Some people, I believe, feel uncomfortable at the knowledge that their obituaries are ready filed in scores of newspaper offices. Others take it philosophically or humorously. I knew one active old gentleman who used to call regularly at a northern newspaper office every couple of years and bring his own obituary notice up to date for them. The great charm, as I say, about writing the obituary of a living friend is that you can at last tell the whole truth about him, which you could not do before, for fear of hurting his feelings. There are people, of course, who object to a critic speaking anything but good of the dead ; they also, by the way, generally object to your saying anything but good of the living. If the poor critic must not tell the truth about the living man because he is living, nor about the dead man because he is dead, the chances for disagreeable truth-telling become painfully limited. I decline to be bound by any such sentimentality; I warn my friends that I have said some horrible things about them in their obituaries—things that would make them dislike me for the rest of their days if I were to publish them now. I see no reason to show these people any consideration when they show me so little. A decent man would recognize that an obituary notice costs the conscientious writer of it a good deal of time and trouble, and he would recognize that the least he can do is to see that all this labour of love is not in vain. Instead of which, most of these people persist in living an unconscionable time after their obituaries have been done, with the result that the critic has to keep adding to them, and in some cases revising his point of view. If I were an editor, I should publish a composer's obituary every three years after he had reached the age of forty-five, whether he were dead or not; if he were not, the plain truths of the notice might make him wish he were. Strauss, for example, is quite dead in all but the merely physical sense; why then should not his obituary as a composer appear as well to-day as twenty years hence? Some of these unthinking people, one is glad to say, get hoist with their own petard; they live on and on until no one knows whether they are dead or alive. Goldmark's death took us all by surprise; we all thought him dead years ago. It was only lately that I discovered that Max Bruch was still alive, aged eighty. Now that I have done a careful obituary of him, he will probably live to be a hundred. But in even worse taste than living on after your obituary is written is dying before it is written. I myself had left Scriabine and Max Reger over because I thought there was no hurry in the case of youngish men like these. They both seized their opportunity when I was off my guard, and died at me without a moment's warning. The moral concept of duty to your biographer is only rudimentarily developed, I am afraid, in musicians.

E

ON INSTRUMENTS AND THEIR PLAYERS

IN his *Overtones* Mr Huneker, the American musical critic, has a delightful essay on "Literary Men who Loved Music." One section of that essay—"Balzac as Music Critic" —gives an account of two of Balzac's less-known but, to musicians, very interesting short stories, *Gambara* and *Massimilla Doni*. Mr Huneker here forestalled me. Years ago, when I was in my teens, I translated both of these stories, but the only publisher to whom I offered the translation stupidly declined it on the ground that he had been informed that the stories were not among Balzac's best. Of course they are not; their interest to-day is not as fiction, but as excellent studies of certain aspects of the musical temperament. Balzac was not a musician, I think; indeed, I seem to remember a passage in one of his letters in which he tells a correspondent how, in order to get inside the skin of these musical characters of his, he used to engage an old pianist to come now and then and play the piano to him—much in the same way that Darwin, having been told by some joker or other that music had an influence on the growth of plants, hired a man to play the trombone for several hours a day to a row of beans. In *Gambara*, Balzac anticipates a good deal of

Wagner and Berlioz. In *Massimilla Doni* he has a fascinating study of an Italian melomaniac whose one passion in life is "to hear a perfect concord between two voices, or between a voice and the first string of the violin." So far as I am aware, this is the only existing study of a type of music-lover we still meet with occasionally, who is interested not so much in music *qua* music as in certain sensuous delights that music can give. I myself know a man who will never, if he can help it, miss a performance of the *Rhinegold*—but all he wants to hear in the opera is the opening chord of E flat, 135 bars long, that depicts the surging Rhine. But I am more immediately reminded of Balzac by another friend of mine in London, who the other day, more in sorrow than in anger, wrote to censure me for the latest nasty thing I had said about the prima donna. My friend loves the prima donna; he would not miss Melba or Patti for anything; and he tells me that my inability to appreciate this kind of thing is a sad defect in my make-up.

My own objection to the prima donna is that, as a rule, she represents merely tone and technique without intelligence. I am sure that some day an American genius will invent an instrument that will be to singing what the pianola is to the piano; and then the prima donna's occupation will be gone. I do not dislike cold perfection in singing, but I give it, I hope, its true place in the scheme of things musical—and that place is necessarily a rather low one. In the human arts, beauty for me is not complete unless coloured and vivified by humanity. It is mainly among the less musical people, I fancy, that the passion for instruments purely as instruments exists. But how little the less musical people are to be trusted in these matters is shown by the inaccuracies of most literary men's references to instruments and their effects. They generally talk in *clichés* when they touch this subject. My admiration for Anatole France is unbounded; I can follow him in most things, but not in his rhapsody upon the flute in *The Revolt of the Angels.* When Nectaire plays that, to me, rather lymphatic instrument, "one seemed to be listening to the nightingale and the Muses singing together, the soul of Nature and the soul of Man. And the old man ordered and developed his thoughts in a musical language full of grace and daring. He told of love, of fear, of vain quarrels, of all-conquering laughter, of the calm light of the intellect, of the arrows of the mind piercing with their golden shafts the monsters of Ignorance and Hate. He told also of Joy and Sorrow bending their twin heads over the earth, and of Desire, which brings worlds into being." I myself have never heard a flute that had half that magical power, and I doubt whether Anatole France has. I surmise that he is thinking of the ideal flute, the poet's flute, not the pale flute of the modern orchestra—the flaxen-haired High School Miss among orchestral instruments. No doubt he is dreaming of the classical flute—the flute of Dionysos—which he

has never heard, but whose effect he imagines to
have been such as he describes. But the Greek
aulos was not at all like the modern flute. It
might more correctly be called a clarinet; and
of the cosmic suggestiveness of the clarinet—the
brunette—we can believe a little more than of
the flute—the anæmic blonde. Of all instruments the flute is intellectually the feeblest. It
should always be played by pale young men in
spectacles, rejoicing in some such gravely comical
name as Tootal. The very manner of playing it
—sideways from the face—is an incitement to
hilarity; no artist would dare to depict an angel
playing the transverse flute.

Instruments, in fact, have distinct personalities,
and each of them should be played by people
born with certain characters and physiques and
bearing appropriate names. The oboe and cor
anglais were meant from the beginning of time
for players with a touch of acridity in their names
—Grice, for example. For the violin, players
should have as many liquid consonants as possible
in their names; Corelli was a happy stroke on
the part of Providence. When we come down
to the larger viola and 'cello we look for the
darker consonants—Klengel, Becker, Popper,
and Piatti are good examples; while for the
double bass a man's name should have still
darker consonants and vowels; Providence did
the right thing, for example, when it made
Bottesini take up that instrument—a jolly lumbering name for a jolly lumbering instrument. The
harp should never be played except by young

ladies with golden hair; and the instrument ought to be barred by statute from all except those named Cecilia, Angelica, or Christina. One of the rare delights of my life is to listen to the saxophone. The instrument seldom appears in our concert rooms, but we can occasionally hear a quartet or a quintet of saxophones at the music halls. For rich, fat, good-natured tone there is nothing to equal it; it is the very soul of good beer made audible, and should have been invented by a German instead of a Belgian. But only Germans ought to play it, and only Germans with names appropriate to the tone of the instrument—ponderous, fleshy names, with a rich Teutonic gurgle in them, such as Humperdinck or Guggenheim or Bugenhagen, names unthinkable in connection with, say, the violin. This affinity between people and instruments is an important one that has never yet received the attention it deserves from philosophers. The elder Disraeli once pointed out how impossible it would be to associate an epic poem with anyone of the name of Titus. Who knows but that the bad orchestral performances we sometimes get are due to the fact that the various instruments are being played by people with the wrong names or the wrong colour of hair?

THE POETS AND ORCHESTRAL INSTRUMENTS

ONE of the musical journals offered, a little while ago, a prize for the best collection of novelists' and poets' "howlers" about music. It is an excellent idea. Many of the older howlers are now current coin in musical circles; but there must be a fine fresh crop of them every year, and someone should see to the annual harvesting of it. Apart from actual howlers, however, an interesting study might be made of what the poets and novelists have written about music. The result of such a study, I think, would be to show that however keenly some of them may enjoy music, few of them hear it *as* music—hear it, that is, as a musician does. (Perhaps this is true of most of the people who attend concerts; they are like Mr Max Beerbohm's delightful Zuleika Dobson, who always used to make the open confession, "I don't know anything about music really, but I know what I like.") I have been set reflecting on the poet's attitude towards music by a charming little poem in the new volume—*Olton Pools*—of my friend, Mr John Drinkwater. The poem took its origin from the tombstone of one Anthony Crundle, "farmer of this parish," and his wife Susan, who died at the ages of eighty-two and eighty-six respectively, after fifty-

three years of wedded life. "He delighted in
music," says the record of old Anthony. Thereupon Mr Drinkwater gives us a delightful little
picture of Anthony and his piccolo, on which,
according to Mr Drinkwater, "he played of a
night to himself and Sue." Now I know Mr
Drinkwater to be fond of music, and more than
fond of, at any rate, one musician—if a mere
musical critic may place himself in that category.
But when next I see Mr Drinkwater I am going
to urge on him the desirability of studying a
book on orchestration, or at least of coming with
me to an orchestral concert and allowing me to
point out the various instruments by sight and
sound. I can see what has happened. He has
pitched upon the piccolo for Anthony Crundle
because of the musical quality not of the instrument but of the word. Our poets, in truth, are
to be commiserated with: as a rule the English
names of musical instruments are neither musical
nor poetic. The one that falls most sweetly
upon the ear is perhaps the lute, which, perhaps
because of its very poetry, has dropped out of
the musical life of to-day. "Flute" does indeed
rhyme roughly with "lute," but to a sensitive ear
it comes no nearer "lute" than "shove" does to
"love," or "snarling" does to "darling." After
"lute," "flute" is a rough-skinned, nerveless,
dead-eyed sort of word. "Viola" comes next in
point of musico-poetic quality. Coleridge made
a gallant attempt, in *The Ancient Mariner*, to
poetize the bassoon ; but I have never been able
to reconcile myself to the word even as he uses

it there. "Bassoon" has the double disadvantage of setting us thinking of "gossoon" and "baboon"—two words that we cannot imagine any really nice poet using. I often wish that Coleridge had made his wedding-guest hear, instead of the bassoon, a poetically-named instrument like the shawm or the tromba marina; though of course the tone of neither of these instruments would have been so valid a reason as that of the bassoon was for the unfortunate man beating his breast.

However much the poets may rhapsodize about musical instruments, they never attempt to rhyme the names of more than one or two of them. Perhaps the lute is oftenest, though still rarely, used for this purpose; Herrick, for instance, rhymes it with "mute." Poets fight shy of the violin: they always have resort to the cowardly subterfuge of "strings," which rhymes with "wings" and "sings," and thus sets going a whole circus of facile poetic sentiments. I cannot imagine "piano" being used as an end-rhyme, except, perhaps, by a cowboy poet, or by one of those painfully vigorous Colonial gentlemen who drop a volume of high-explosive verse on us now and then; they would no doubt rhyme it, in their racy, naturalistic way, with "guano." I can imagine the quandary Mr Drinkwater would have been in had Anthony Crundle's favourite instrument been specifically indicated on his tombstone. I have a vision of Mr Drinkwater, pale but determined, wrestling with such lines as these—

> "He sang his love on the tenor trumpet,
> And suffering Susan had to lump it";

or these—

> "He played a scale on the muted horn,
> And Susan wished she were dead and gorn—
> Wished, indeed, she'd never been born."

Perhaps, on the whole, it is as well that poets do not try experiments of this kind. Matthew Arnold, in *The Punishment of Marsyas*, has probably achieved a record by introducing the names of no fewer than three musical instruments as end-rhymes; but the effect cannot be called dazzling. The lyre comes out not so badly; but it is rather weak to rhyme "flutes" twice with "roots" ("pine-wooded roots" and "torn up by the roots"); while the poet surely indulges in more than the normal poetic license when he speaks thus of the Maenads—

> "Each her ribboned tambourine
> Flinging on the mountain-sod,
> With a lovely frightened mien
> Came about the youthful god."

If the Maenads really used tambourines, which I take leave to doubt, it is pretty certain they were not be-ribboned. In any case, on the poet's own admission, Apollo

> "turned his beauteous face
> Haughtily another way";

and I am not surprised. Apollo, though he had no technical training in music, was a cultivated aristocratic amateur ; and one can hardly imagine him taking up with tambourine players.

I am afraid the truth is that our poets have not a very precise sense of the tone and colour of orchestral instruments, and still less of the blended effects of them. Tennyson, in *Maud*, speaks of the dance-music at the Hall being played on the flute, violin and bassoon—a truly appalling combination. Can any poet, indeed, represent to himself at will the tone of any given instrument as a musician can? The poet can visualize, say, a rose and a lily, and is in no danger of confusing the appearance of the two. But I doubt whether any poet can hear internally, whenever he likes, the oboe tone or the clarinet tone, and differentiate the one from the other as easily and as surely as he can the sight or scent of the rose from that of the lily. The poets use the names of instruments simply as conventional emotional counters, one of which is just as good for their purpose as another. There is no reason, that is to say, why a poet should use in a given line "lyre" instead of "flute," or "flute" instead of "lyre"; it is merely that in the one case he wants a rhyme for "higher" and in the other case for "root." Yet how glorious it would be if some poet with a genuinely musical ear could incarnate for us the soul of each instrument in a line or two as surely as he can give us the form and colour of a tree, a river, or a sunset! And why should the poets be content to give even to their verbal counters only the conventional values they have had for ages? Why

do they not learn something of those characteristic modern tone-effects that are to the musician
what the discovery of a quite new colour would
be to the painter?   When a poet speaks, for
example, of the trumpet, it is always with the
implication that the trumpet is a noisy, martial,
blood-stirring instrument.   He does not know
that modern soft trumpet-and-trombone harmony
is one of the most ravishingly beautiful effects
that mortal ears could wish to savour.   Nor
does he know, apparently, the strange, remote,
half-sweet half-acrid, attenuated colour of the
muted as distinguished from the open trumpet.
Yes, we shall decidedly have to start orchestral
classes for poets and novelists.   When Mr
Drinkwater had worked through the wood-wind
section he would know that had Anthony played
the piccolo every evening he would never have
lived to be eighty-two.   Susan would have
poisoned him in the first year of their married
life.

THE ELASTIC LANGUAGE—I

OF all the wonders of all the arts, surely harmony in music is the most wonderful. It may be that some day each of the other arts will be brought to a standstill from the sheer impossibility of putting to new uses the material that in the course of many centuries will have been manipulated in every conceivable manner. Architecture and sculpture, perhaps, will be the first to give out: there must be some natural limit to the possible number of vital permutations and combinations of straight lines and curves, and it may not be too fantastic to believe that the circle of really new things to be said in these two arts is steadily shrinking from generation to generation. Of painting I will not venture to speak; but in poetry and prose there is even now an unmistakable impatience on the part of criticism with everything that does not justify its existence by being something quite different from everything of its kind that has appeared before; and there must surely be a limit to the number of changes that can be rung upon words, upon the ten or a dozen elemental emotions that are the substance of all artistic thinking, and upon the few standard patterns upon which all plots are constructed. But to musical novelty no man can see an end, because the language of music is not a fixed but a fluid one. I am aware that an English philosopher used to be haunted in his youth by the idea that before long music would reach the limit of its resources, because there are only thirteen notes in the octave, and thirteen digits are capable of only a certain number of permutations and combinations. But he forgot, in the first place, that what may be called the extensive material of music—the mere number of digits spread out, as it were, on a table—is not thirteen notes only, but as many multiples of thirteen as there are octaves in our instruments or our orchestras. That fact of itself enormously increases the mathematical possibilities of the scale. The intensive resources of music also are seemingly illimitable. They are of two orders. Not only do the many timbres of our instruments permit of an infinite rearrangement of colours, but we are just beginning to realize that colour in music has, in addition to its aural quality, a quasi-spatial quality. That is to say, we are now learning to use colour not exclusively on the flat, as in the older music, but in depths of foreground and background. A combination of tones on the pianoforte, for instance, that sounds hideously discordant when all the notes are played with equal force, may take on a curious beauty when some of the upper notes, let us say, are played *pianissimo* against a *forte* in the left hand. Debussy in his later work has made some very interesting experiments in this "spacing" of piano colour. The problem is one not merely of the different timbres of the various registers of the piano, but of the over-tones in the harmonies.   Since each note sounded is not merely the note we call C or G or A, but is accompanied by all the harmonics of itself, while each of these harmonics in turn generates harmonics of its own, it is evident that every chord is accompanied by an almost infinite number of satellite tones, ranging from the bass of the chord to the top of the piano scale.   At present our theory in these things is stronger than our practice.   We know that all these satellite tones are there, but in actual hearing we can distinguish only one or two of them, and that only by a conscious effort of the ear and brain.   But there can be little doubt that our hearing for overtones will become more acute in the course of time ; and when it is fairly well developed, a whole new field of harmonic effect will be opened to composers. Tenuous high notes can be used to reinforce subtly the main harmonics of the basic harmony, or, by stressing some of the harmonics that are, as we say, slightly out of tune, we can give fascinating piquancy to the flavour of the chord. It was along this line that Debussy experi-mented.   It is clear that it will open up to music a field of harmonic resource as vast as that opened up for the art by Monteverde and the others who first began to use unprepared discords as a positive, instead of a negative, element in the harmonic palette.

But my concern to-day is not with these developments of the future, but with the other

intensive resource of music with which history
has made us familiar—harmony as a language
that, instead of remaining fixed, as a spoken
language becomes after a certain time, is infinitely elastic both in its vocabulary and in
the combinations of that vocabulary. We shall
best appreciate this advantage of music, perhaps,
by seeing how greatly the expressive resources
of the spoken language would be increased
could words undergo that rearrangement of
their letters that the notes of a chord can undergo. Everyone will remember the delicious
mistake of the typist (or compositor) who a
few weeks ago made Mr J. C. Squire speak
of Mr Hotario Bottomley. That is the verbal
equivalent of a change in the distribution of the
notes in a chord: the thing is not the same,
and yet it is the same. Now if we could consistently manipulate the letters of words in this
way, rearranging them, adding or omitting one
or two, we could create new words that would
abbreviate and concentrate expression by combining two images in the one symbol. At
present we only discover these rearrangements
by the mistakes of compositors and others. A
typist of mine once wrote "platitune" for "platitude." Here, I think, is a word that might well
be incorporated into the language. A platitune
would be a platitudinous melody, Two concepts
would be simultaneously expressed by the one
symbol. Let us take another case. The other
day, passing a surgery, I noticed that owing to
the lapse of the initial letter the place was

described as an "urgery." It struck me that here again is a word that our language would be all the richer for. When the policeman brought a Saturday night accident case into the hospital, the surgeon could say, "Take him to the urgery," thus conveying, in the minimum of words, the double fact that it was a matter for surgery and that the case was urgent. A little while ago, one of the correspondents at the Front, who had intended to speak of our men as having overcome a weakened German resistance, was made to say that they overcame a "weakneed" German resistance. If the word "weak-kneed" had not already been in existence, here would have been a chance to adopt it: yet our purists, who would raise no objection to increasing the resources of the language by hyphenating "weak" and "kneed" into a double-barrelled word, would protest against such a telescoping of the two as we get in "weakneed," that, from its mere spelling, lets us know that the German resistance was not merely weak, but weaker than it once was—again a duality of concept expressed in a single term.

If words, instead of being the inelastic things they are at present, were as elastic as the constituent elements of musical harmony, we should not only be able to endow the same letters with many new meanings; often the new word would set us upon the track of a new truth. Let us suppose that a musician is improvising at the piano, or even playing a piece already written. In the last chord he

F

strikes a wrong note. What does he do, if he is a man of resource? Instead of rising from the piano stool in confusion, or making matters worse by hastily playing the right chord after the wrong one, thus advertising his error, he calmly accepts the wrong chord as the starting-point for a new train of thought, and improvises until it suits him to revert to the original idea. It is on record that Liszt or someone actually did this at a recital, and, of course, only those who knew thoroughly the work he was playing were aware that anything had gone wrong. And in the process of composing on paper, something in a man's brain will make him unconsciously put down a combination that was not the one he had been consciously working up to, but that sets him off on a train of thought that opens out new possibilities for his original idea. Let me now give what I take to be an equivalent of this process in the language of words. When the War broke out, I wrote an article in the *Musical Times* in which I pointed out that a great war was always a liberator of a new nervous energy, the chances being that the energy would have a touch of disease in it. I instanced the early French Romantics, many of whom attributed their own excessively excitable nervous systems to the fact that they were born during the convulsions of the Napo-leonic wars. "What else can you expect of us," said Alfred de Musset, "conceived as we were between two battles?" This came out in my proof, "conceived as we were between two bottles." This was a new light on the subject for me ; and I thought the emendation so much nearer the probable truth than the original that I asked the editor of the *Musical Times* to let the error stand. Dr McNaught was compelled to decline, on the ground that they had some clergymen among their subscribers. Now if words were harmonies, and literature what music is, this printer's error would have been not an error but a discovery. From it a whole new thesis could have been developed, as Liszt developed a new piece of music out of a wrong note struck accidentally.

THE ELASTIC LANGUAGE—II

IT is because harmony is not only a language but the most elastic of languages that it cannot be taught. What passes for harmony teaching in schools and text-books is not harmony teaching at all, but the teaching of harmonic analysis. The tradition is kept up that there is a grammar of harmony that students can and must learn; but that tradition survives only because teachers can use it to their own profit. Harmony teaching is not an art but an industry, and a highly profitable industry to the professors, the schools, and the writers of text-books. They tell the students that it is essential they should learn, while they are young, the grammar of harmony. But there is no grammar of harmony. Grammar is only a set of rules by which all the members of a community speaking a common language agree, for convenience sake, to be bound. It may be said that the main rules of grammar are necessarily the same in all languages—that the agreement of the noun with its verb, for instance, is not an artificial but a natural relation, a basic necessity for intelligible expression because it is a basic necessity of coherent thinking. But the different languages show different rules for the agreement of noun and verb: in Greek, plural neuter nouns take a singular verb; in Russian, the genitive is used instead of the accusative after a negation; and so on. Any rule whatever, however irrational it may seem, will work perfectly well so long as everyone agrees to abide by it. But there are no such "rules" in harmony, and no "grammar" in the sense that word carries in connection with language. The text-books tell the guileless student that this or that is "correct" or "incorrect," "good" or "bad"; but the truth is that anything is correct and good that sounds so. There is perhaps not an example in the text-books of what the student is warned to avoid as "bad" that could not be shown to be a constituent of some excellent effect in someone or other's music. There is, I repeat, no body of accepted practice that can be taught as the "grammar" of harmony. All that the text-books are useful for is to teach harmonic analysis. Just as the text-book of prosody tells the student what spondees and dactyls are, and teaches him to recognize a hexameter or an iambic pentameter metre when he sees one, so the harmony books can tell him that a certain combination of notes is the second inversion of the chord of the dominant seventh; but just as no amount of knowledge of prosody will help anyone in the slightest degree to make poetry unless he is a poet, so no amount of knowledge of text-book harmony will teach anyone who is not a born harmonist to think harmonically; and just as a poet could weave the subtlest rhythmical patterns without ever having even heard of the terms dactyl or spondee, so a born musician can write abstruse harmony without being able to name a number of the chords that he uses instinctively.

If the writing of harmony, indeed, had been dependent upon the theory of harmony, we should have very little music to-day, for the plain truth is that there is *no* theory of harmony. There is any amount of theories of harmony, but there is not a single theory, as Dr Shirlaw shows in the remarkably sound and learned volume that he has recently published,[1] that has won, or is likely to win, general acceptance. Dr Shirlaw, who has an incomparable knowledge of his subject, passes in review the chief theoretical treatises on harmony that have appeared in Europe since the sixteenth century. I cordially and maliciously commend the book to the attention of all teachers and students— particularly to the former, who, by the time they have reached its 484th page, will, if they are honest with themselves, have grave doubts as to the truth of many of the things they have been telling their pupils with the air of a revelation from heaven. If the use of harmony as a language had been in any way dependent on a knowledge on the composers' part of the nature of the material they were manipulating, music could never have been written. Attempts have been made to deduce our scales and harmonies from the harmonic series thrown off by a vibrating

[1] *The Theory of Harmony: An Enquiry into the Natural Principles of Harmony, with an Examination of the Chief Systems of Harmony from Rameau to the Present Day;* by Matthew Shirlaw, Mus.D., F.R.C.O. Novello & Co.

string or a sounding pipe; but at some point or other—the justification of the minor harmony, for example—each demonstrator has either become hopelessly entangled in contradictions, or has had to call in metaphysics to fill the gap that acoustics could not bridge. Theory has always failed utterly to explain the practice of its own day. The seventeenth and eighteenth century composers, who were also theorists, were constantly using chords rightly and accounting for them wrongly. Thinking, as they had been taught to do by the theorists of the past, in terms of intervals rather than of chords, they tied themselves into the most ludicrous knots of analysis because they could not perceive that this or that chord was simply the inversion of another. In our own day we have seen a leading theorist—the late Ebenezer Prout—issue a text-book of harmony based on a certain acoustical theory (which text-book was largely used in schools), and then, in a new edition of the work, throw over the former theory and formulate a new one, which, however, as Dr Shirlaw shows, is no more consistent, no more capable of explaining the facts, than the old one was; and the new text-book, faulty as it is, in turn becomes gospel to thousands of innocent teachers and students.

A popular theory is that harmony has been evolved from melody. It could be argued with equal, perhaps superior, force that melody has been evolved from harmony: that is to say, man did not first invent a scale and then discover

how to make harmonies from it, but a sub-
conscious feeling for harmony—a feeling it may
have taken thousands of years to develop—
guided him in the construction of the scale.
Nothing in the whole history of the subject is
more remarkable than the way in which the
unconscious instincts of men have guided them
to the truth of harmony where the reasoning of
the theorists would have led them away from it.
The folk singer who was irresistibly attracted
to the third of the scale, by reason of its
peculiarly satisfactory relation to the tonic,
at a time when theorists were maundering about
the abstract virtues of the fourth and fifth, had
not the slightest inkling that he was acoustically
justified in his preference (the third being
sounded as the first harmonic after the octave
and the fifth in every tone that man or instrument can make); he merely obeyed an instinct.
It may almost be said that he was not so much
using harmony as harmony was using him. So
has it always been. The interval of the tritone
(the augmented fourth), against which the
mediæval theorists fulminated as the theologians
did against the devil, came gradually and
unconsciously to be recognized (as the essence
of the flavour of the chord of the dominant
seventh) as one of the seminal factors in modern
harmony.

THE ELASTIC LANGUAGE—III

HARMONY as a language owes its wonderful elasticity to the fact that it is a natural language—the only truly natural language that man has ever spoken. All other languages are arbitrary: there is not the slightest reason in nature why we should call a dog a dog or a cat a cat, or why nouns should be declined and verbs conjugated in the way they are. But harmony is not an invented or a manufactured language but a natural language. It is not so much we who speak it as nature that speaks it through us. It is the universal thing it is, conveying the same concepts, embodying the same logic, to all the nations that after a long process of evolution have learned how to limit and simplify their melodic scales, because nature herself has given us, in the overtones and undertones of each musical sound, the basic material of our music —a material that is necessarily the same where-ever there are sounds and ears to hear them.

Man, that is to say, is by nature a harmonic animal just as he is by nature an ambulatory or an ethical animal. All the grace and ease and variety of his present movements, all the subtleties and nobilities of his present ethical sense, are only the coming into visible being of certain potentialities that were in him from the first. Harmony has no more developed at haphazard than a tree has. Its actual historical evolution, indeed, has been precisely like that of a tree: from some two or three chords that were and are the trunk of music there have grown, step by step, all the chords in use to-day; and chords that at one time seemed to be twigs thrown off from a branch have in the course of generations become in their turn substantial branches, from which have sprung still smaller branches, from which again have come seemingly isolated and final twigs that in turn, we may be sure, will become parent stems of still other twigs. It is a pity that someone does not write a real history of harmony. Mr Charles Macpherson has just attempted something of the kind in an excellent little volume published by Messrs Kegan Paul & Co.[1]; but the subject deserves a more extended treatment. It would be interesting to have the pedigrees of all the most complicated chords of to-day traced back through one ancestor after another to their first parent, and the passage in this or that composer's work signalized in which it makes its first significant appearance. A genealogical tree of this kind would not only have its historical value. It would also show how supremely natural a language harmony is, and how it owes the universality of its meaning to the fact that through all the ages, in man *qua* man, sound *qua* sound has been incessantly striving to realize in detail its own primal

[1] *A Short History of Harmony*. The Music-Lover's Library, 1s. 6d. net.

dynamic force, as a tree strives to realize in trunk and branch and twig and leaf the primal dynamic force concentrated in its seed.

I referred in my last article to the fallacy that will be found in so many treatises on music—that man began by making scales, and having written for a long time melodies in these scales, found that certain notes were agreeable when sounded together, and so was led by slow stages to the discovery of harmony. It is only historically and externally that melody precedes harmony : psychologically, it is hardly too much to say, harmony has from the first—even before harmony was written—been man's guide in the making of his scales and his melodies. Harmony, it would seem, has always been working sub-consciously in him ; and the history of harmony is the history of the sub-conscious emerging further and further into consciousness. Without the scale we now use, harmony of any extended range and complexity would be impossible ; and we can hardly doubt that the process described in the histories, by which the Greek and the mediæval scales have insensibly settled into the modern scale, was at bottom the effort of man's sub-conscious harmonic sense to find an outlet— much in the same way that a tuber, in a dark room, unconsciously throws out feelers towards the chink through which comes a ray of light. The mediæval musicians, in their constant manipulations of the ecclesiastical scales so as to get a semitone before the final of the mode, and so on, were unconsciously obeying an

obscure harmonic "pull" within them towards
the perfect cadence, and towards the dominant-
tonic relationship that is the basis of modern
tonality and of modern music. It is a fact of
unshakable significance that the basic elements
of our music—the three or four trunks, as it
were, from which the forest has grown—are
given us in the relations of the first few overtones
of the harmonic series. Long before science
had an inkling of that fact, the musical sense in
man was unconsciously making use of it ; and
for a long period the great masters of polyphonic music wove their beautiful tissues out
of the simple chord-groups suggested by these
elementary relationships. Even to-day, with our
harmony the bold, free thing that it is, there is
no escape, so far as we can see, from the
original bonds that nature has laid upon us.
The importance of the fifth and the fourth in
our modern tonality is apparently the inevitable
outcome of the importance of the fifth and the
fourth in the harmonic series ; and one of the
reasons why the so-called "whole-tone" scale is
so intractable to the larger uses is the absence
from it of these essential pivotal points upon
which the harmony can swing and return without
losing itself.

As Mr Macpherson shows, the bulk of our
serviceable modern harmony has been evolved
from simpler and still simpler elements by three
main processes—(1) the *contraction* of the steps
by which the seminal chords normally follow
each other, (2) an *expansion* of these steps, (3)

chromatic distortion, for which, perhaps, "chromatic sophistication" would be a better term, for it implies simply the subtilization of plain chords by chromatic alteration, the altered forms becoming in their turn diatonic elements in other, and, at first sight, unrelated keys. In Mr Macpherson's little book will be found a demonstration of the historical processes by which some of our seemingly complex modern harmonies have thus been evolved from simple germs. And in this evolution we seem to see the same unconscious forces at work as in the organic world. Rich as she is in varieties, nature is chiefly interested in the type. Oddities appear and disappear, being infertile. The record of harmonic evolution is strewn with innovations that came to nothing because they were too far removed from the main line of life of the time to be successfully grafted upon it. What I have ventured to call by the name of "serviceable harmony,"— harmony, that is to say, that is sufficiently malleable and flexible for contemporary musical thought to do whatever it likes with it—has always come about by gradual and logical development from pre-existing harmony, not by a sudden leap from it. In our own day we have seen the limitations of freak harmony demonstrated by Debussy and Scriabine; their systems, admirable as they are for special purposes, are not generally serviceable for all that a modern composer of comprehensive genius has to say; and for the full utilization of them we shall have to wait until the really vital parts of them have been absorbed into the general body of harmony, and become a natural, unconscious language for all musicians. The process of evolution by which new relationships are always being established between the basic elements of harmony is most aptly illustrated in Wagner, and, in a smaller degree, in Strauss. The harmonies of *Tristan* are for the most part nothing more than natural and inevitable sophistications of the simpler harmonies of earlier music. That is why, in spite of their novelty, any ordinarily musical person could follow them without difficulty ; and it is because Wagner derives all his twigs and leaves from a basic trunk or two that there is not a single harmony in the whole of his music that has not justified itself and become part of the current musical tongue of the world. Strauss sometimes wastes himself in experiments that are doomed to infertility ; but he also has expanded the harmonic idiom in just the way that Wagner did : the best of his novel harmonies "argue out" logically because they are only sophistications of simpler combinations. And the sign of the great man is that, as with Wagner and Strauss, he is the master of his own harmony, instead of being the servant of it, as Debussy and Scriabine often are. The harmonic innovations in *Tristan* were not spirits that Wagner had raised but could not lay again. His thought moves freely and naturally among them ; they came into being ready clothed with the new melodic and rhythmic figuration that was most appropriate to them, whereas Debussy has had to give up in despair the problem of fusing his new harmony into an indivisible whole with his melody and his rhythm—especially the latter. These experimentalists do invaluable service in suggesting possible fields of new harmonic subtlety which it will be the business of more broadly-based composers to cultivate; but the great stream of real progress—if I may alter the metaphor without becoming Hibernian—will always flow along the main bed that time has channelled so deep. If any of us lives another fifty years, it will be interesting to see the result when a new harmonic sophistication gives us something as much subtler than *Tristan* as *Tristan* is subtler than *Figaro*. It may be that in time, as some hold, the limits of the possibilities of our present scale will be reached, and composers will have to resort to quarter-tones; but judging from the past, it will be many generations yet before the last change has been rung upon the thirteen notes of the scale from which all the music we know has grown.

RECIPES

THE sensation of the month has been the discovery by a writer in the *Musical Times* that Mr Bantock is a Scotsman—not, as we all thought, a descendant of the Caliphs and the Lights of the Harem. Mr Hugh S. Roberton, the maker of this discovery, that will send his name down to posterity along with those of Roger Bacon, Newton, Darwin and Ignatius Donnelly, holds that as Mr Bantock's "grandmother was a Munro," and "his father was born in Sutherlandshire," the composer simply could not help writing Scottish music—whatever that may be. The sceptical may say that all that Mr Bantock has done is to base a symphony on Hebridean folk-songs, and that to do this a man no more needs to have Scottish blood in him than Brahms needed to be a Magyar to write Hungarian dances, or Bizet needed to be a Spaniard in order to write *Carmen*. Mr Bantock, in truth, seems to have had some doubt as to the power of his ancestral Scotticism to bear up against a lifetime devoted to Turkish delight and sherbet. No doubt he had an uneasy feeling that the blood of the Munro was thinning a little in him, and that even the racial virtue of having a father born in Sutherlandshire eighty years or so ago could not remain unimpaired for ever. So, according to Mr Roberton, the composer, "with characteristic thoroughness and big capacity, surrounded himself at his English home with all things Scottish. And now, if it is there you will be finding yourself some day, it is the Celtic song and the Celtic story you will hear, and the skirl of the pipes and the dancing to the Highland tunes forbye. And where this music is written, there are ever the sweet-smelling bog-myrtle and the heather on the table, and the fire that gives warmth in the room is not one of Lowland coal, but of Highland peat. A thorough Celt is Bantock."

I greatly like this idea of getting the authentic Celtic atmosphere in brassy Birmingham by means of what the stage hands would call "properties." If the Munro cannot get to the heather, obviously the heather—or as much of it as the florist has in stock—must be made to come to the Munro. It is to be hoped, too, that Mr Bantock, when he was writing the symphony, had an adequate supply of Highland peat; one can dimly imagine how disastrous it would have been to the Celticism of the music had a servant, in the composer's absence, fed the waning fire with a bucketful of Lowland coal. "Get drunk," was Baudelaire's advice to the young artist. "Whether with wine, or women, or art does not matter; but get drunk." Mr Bantock is evidently as grimly bent on getting Celtic as some people are on getting drunk and other people on getting salvation. But I do not blame him. I admire him, in fact, for what Mr Roberton calls his "characteristic thoroughness." For if Macready

G

used to work himself into a passion, before going
on the stage for one of his great scenes, by
furiously shaking a ladder, why should not a
composer take a mild botanical stimulant
occasionally for the sake of "national atmosphere," or, if he is describing the deeds of
heroes, whistle softly to keep up his own
courage?

I was so struck by the ingenuity of Mr
Bantock's devices for keeping up the Celtic
pressure of his blood that it occurred to me
that other composers might have fortified themselves in analogous ways for the writing of this
or that work. So I wrote to a few of them,
asking them if they would be good enough, in
the interests of psychology, to favour me with any
information on the subject that might be made
public without indelicacy. I am glad to say
that quite a number of them have responded
cordially, though considerations of space make
it impossible for me to avail myself here of all
the valuable data they have placed at the service
of science.

Sir Edward Elgar writes: "I have long
practised in secret the methods which, I now
hear with interest, are cultivated by my friend
Bantock. When I was writing the *Sea Pictures*
I made sure of getting the right briny atmosphere by giving up meat for an exclusively fish
diet, and by having a bath of Tidman's sea salt
twice a day. When I was composing *Polonia*
I lived for a month on polony sausage, under
the pardonable delusion that this was the

national diet of the Poles. I discovered my error too late to prevent a slight trace of a German accent appearing here and there in the music among so much that is genuinely Polish."

Richard Strauss says : " Certainly ! I will tell you how I wrote the first scene of *Elektra*, and that will show you the benefit of going straight to nature for your inspiration. In order to find out what Elektra might be supposed to have thought and felt when she was a badly-used servant in the house of Aegisthus, I had an under-housemaid—a poor, half-witted creature from the Black Forest— chained to a post at the end of the garden, and touched up occasionally by the village children with whips and sticks. I had all their yells carefully recorded on giant gramophones, and the opening scene of my opera is the result. It was only after several experiments with a guillotine and a number of dear friends who are now mysteriously missing that I was able to find just the right music to accompany the execution of Jochanaan ; and of course during the composition of *The Legend of Joseph* I smoked none but Egyptian cigarettes." The letter concludes with a message to Sir Edgar Speyer that has been made virtually illegible by the Censor.

Debussy says that the resources of medical and dietetic science were strained to the utmost to induce the desired degree of chlorosis in the schoolgirls who sat to him as models for *Mélisande* and *The Blessed Damozel*. He wrote

Jardins sous la pluie in goloshes and a mackintosh, with an open umbrella in his left hand.

During the composition of his famous Welsh Rhapsody, Mr Edward German ate nothing but Welsh rarebits, drank nothing but Welsh ale, and slept with a copy of *Wild Wales* under his pillow.

Stravinsky says that he only succeeded in getting such a wonderful Chinese atmosphere in *Le Rossignol* by eating chow-chow every hour, growing a pigtail, and having himself lacquered all over.

Sir Charles Stanford writes: "I am a firm believer in this sort of suggestion. When I was writing my *Wellington* Ode I read Napier every morning before breakfast, and slept in Wellington boots. This was rather uncomfortable; but the true artist falters at no sacrifice where his art is concerned. As a preparation for the justly admired Mad Scene of Tilburina in my new opera I brought myself to the verge of imbecility by a prolonged course of reading of the best English musical criticism. Parry tells me, too, that though the family boggled at his introducing wild rats into the house, he kept a colony of white mice when he was writing *The Pied Piper of Hamelin*. Between ourselves, this may account for the tameness of the music. But, of course, not a word of this to Parry." (I need hardly assure Sir Charles that any confidences with which he may honour me are sacred.)

All this seems conclusive enough : but a letter I found on my desk this morning, apparently dropped from nowhere, disturbs the theory somewhat. It is written in a beautiful script, and signed "Ihr ergebenster R.W." It is a little violent in tone here and there, but I have softened the harsher expressions in translation. The letter runs thus: "All nonsense! I have no patience with the idiots who invent theories like this. He must be a poor artist who needs to have his inspiration whipped up by such infantile dodges. As a matter of fact, it isn't the subject or the atmosphere that work up the music, but the music struggling for birth in the composer—how generated he does not know himself—that unconsciously lights upon the subject, and then the atmosphere comes of itself. It is of desire, not possession, that music, like love, is born. If I had wanted to write a Scotch symphony I should neither have gone on a *Rundreise* through Scotland nor sat at home in a Scotch cap and plaid : I should have lived unhappily in ugly London, and hungered for the never-seen Scotland with all the force of my starving soul. These amateur psychologists all begin at the wrong end. The fools who write my biography imagine that I wrote *Tristan* because I was in love with Frau Wesendonck. The truth is that I was in love with Frau Wesendonck because I was writing *Tristan*. Any other other young and reasonably pretty woman with a good figure and a better income would have done as well; but

Mathilde just happened to be there. You must go by contraries where the artist is concerned. It was when I was too poor and too ill to indulge in the voluptuousnesses I loved that I conceived the music of the Venusberg; and I got the key to Parsifal's renunciation of the flesh when I was sating my own. It is not what he has seen that the true artist describes, but the land of heart's desire, as you English say, that he longs to see, but fears he never will see." After this the writer becomes metaphysical, etymological, biological, and tautological, so I cut his communication short.

I make no pretence to deciding between these rival views as to the origin of musical inspiration. I simply give the data, and leave the judgment upon them to the experts.

ON MUSICAL SURGERY

P EOPLE with an eye for the parallelisms
of art and science must have been struck,
as I was, by a paragraph that recently
appeared in one of the London papers, describing the "plastic surgery" that is now being
applied in the Cambridge Hospital to our
wounded soldiers. "In each instance," says
the report, "the state of a patient's face upon
admission is compared" [by means of plaster
casts, coloured drawings, and photographs] "with
the picture it presented when discharged from
hospital ; and it is of interest to note that the
surgeons' aims are the restoration of the features
by means of sound surgical procedure, and only
in very extreme cases is resort made to the
employment of artificial features. The science
of facial plastic surgery implies the building up
of the features and restoration of contour from
the patients' own tissues. Portions of skin,
bone, and cartilage are to-day transferred and
manipulated in a manner which a few months
ago was regarded as an impossibility."

When I read this, I reflected sadly on the
unevenness with which the rewards and the
gratitude of this world are distributed. Here
are surgeons getting their names in the papers,
and being patted on the back by all sorts of
admiring hands, for doing—what ? Nothing,
after all, but what the musical critic has long

been doing in his own particular sphere, without earning anything more than a few ha'pence and a disagreeable plenitude of kicks. The composer and the performer regard the critic as a mere fault-finder who earns a dishonest and precarious livelihood by picking holes in other men's work—better men's work, as they would say in their modest fashion. In reality, the critic is simply the surgeon who, when reluctantly compelled to do so, locates for his patient the patch of diseased tissue in a limb, and suggests the operation that might eliminate it. Creation (or interpretation) and criticism are only the give-and-take of what ought to be a quite friendly discussion upon ends to be achieved and the precise degree to which they have been achieved in a given case. The artist claims to have done so-and-so; the critic invites him to a banquet of wit at which the question of whether the artist has really done so-and-so can be discussed. The artist may complain that it is too often a supper like that of Polonius, "not where he eats, but where he is eaten"; but even so he can have the satisfaction of a double meaning when he calls the critic, as he so often does, a worm.

In a sense there is even more justification for musical than for bodily surgery. For the plain man who, after an accident to his face, goes into the hospital to see what can be done for him, does not begin by denying his plainness. He does not insist, as a preliminary to any dealings between the surgeon and himself, that the surgeon shall admit he is as beautiful as Apollo ; and he does not write angry letters to the surgeon's employers if that postulate has not been taken for granted The great trouble with the artist—under which term I include composer and interpreter—is that, while obviously in need, to the trained observant eye, of a little plastic surgery, he will not have any doubts cast on his claim to be Apollo. He enters for a beauty competition, and insists in advance that the judges are to give him the first prize. Nothing could be done in the Cambridge Hospital with patients who talked like this ; and nothing can be none with the artist until he recognizes that the critic is a being sent to him by a kindly Providence to save him, in many cases, from himself, and to help him, by a little plastic surgery, to restore or improve certain lineaments that are obviously suffering from wear and tear. It is the business of the critic to teach the composer, not how to compose, indeed, but how not to compose. The best teachers of composition admit that composition cannot be taught. That was the conclusion reached, for instance, in Sir Charles Stanford's book on the subject— one of the very best of its kind. We can no more teach a young man how to write music than we can teach him how to write poetry. We can provide him with a certain technique that he must afterwards alter or expand to suit his own way of thinking ; but the way of thinking must be his own, and nothing that the teacher can do can help him here. All that the

teacher can do is to examine the finished product
and say, out of the fund of his richer experience
of art, where it is clumsily worked, where it is
muddled, where it fails in that steady procession
from premises to conclusion that all good art
ought to show, and so on. And purely in this
negative sense the skilled critic can obviously
teach the composers—even the best of them—
a good deal about composition. It would pay
every composer, I think, to have near him some
critic, friendly, but not too friendly, who would
tell him in all frankness when he had done
something stupid, or careless, or conventional,
or feeble. Such a friend might have told Bach
that now and then his piano works were not
so much finished as merely terminated ; no
doubt Anna Magdalena was calling Johann
Sebastian to supper, or there was a rehearsal
at St Thomas's, or Philip Emmanuel was
tugging at papa's coat tails, begging him to go
for a walk ; and so the great man knit his brows,
and, conscious of having still a great deal to say
on the subject of his themes, brought his dis-
course to a summary close. Such a friend
would have told Beethoven or Brahms when
he was becoming too mechanical, too text-
bookish, in his "working-out"—in that always
awkward moment, for example, of transition
from the exposition section to the development
section. Such a friend would have warned
Wagner that he was weakening a passage by a
gross excess of sequential repetition, or that
he was over-loading the *Ring* by telling the

tale four or five times over, and that it would
be better for him in the long run to scrap
his shapeless scheme and build it up again
organically from a single cell. Other friends
of the same enlightened sort would tell Debussy
when the whole-tone scale had exhausted its
welcome; would advise Ravel to cut out the
present alternative section of the Pavane and
write another that should be more worthy of
the rest; would warn this English composer
that piety was a poor substitute for inspiration,
even in the British oratorio; another, that he
was in danger of exploiting to death a certain
sequence of descending chromatic harmonies;
another, that a certain sort of bogus polyphony
was beginning to reveal all too plainly its
complete absence of a secret; another, that in
order to write a Wagnerian opera it is necessary
to be a Wagner; and so on and so on. In all
these cases the critic would be the plastic
surgeon. He could say, with perfect truth,
that *his* science also "implies the building up
of the features and restoration of contour from
the patient's own tissues"; and if, as at the
Cambridge Hospital, "in each instance the state
of a patient's face upon admission is compared
with the picture it presented when discharged
from hospital," I think the composer, as he
looked at himself in the glass after his discharge,
would generally have reason to congratulate
himself. Bach, for example, leaving his plastic-
surgical friend's house with a score of the
Matthew Passion or the B minor Mass under

his arm from which all the mere piously dull
numbers had been excised, would be much like
the patient who had left his warts and his
bunions in the operating room. Strauss would
feel as much better after his scores had been
denuded of all their superfluous notes as the
dropsical patient does after being tapped, or as the
fat and sluggish man after the Turkish bath; or,
to get back to plastic surgery, what could not a
skilled musical surgeon do to correct the hideous
squint and grimace of the *Symphonia Domestica*? The soul of us, surely, as well as the
body of us, needs a periodical setting right; it
certainly needs dexterous manipulation when
something radical has gone wrong. If a man
with a twisted jaw has to go into a hospital to
have it put straight, should there not be a sort
of musical hospital into which Schönberg could
go to be treated for the last piano works and
the *Five Orchestral Pieces*, a hydro in which
Debussy and Ravel could have the sevenths
and ninths got out of their system, or an operating ward in which Strauss could be cut up for
The Legend of Joseph?

QUOTATION IN MUSIC

THERE is a joke in *The Tales of Hoffmann* that invariably passes over the head of an English audience, because of its imperfect education in music. Soon after the entry of Hoffmann and Nicklaus in the first scene, Nicklaus ironically describes his companion as "Never resting day or night" in the pursuit of his amours—nor permitting Nicklaus to rest. The audience catches the words, but probably only the professional musicians know that the music to which Nicklaus sings the words is a quotation from the aria in *Don Giovanni* in which Leporello describes the fatigues *he* has to undergo because of the indefatigable pursuit of women by his master the Don. In Italy, France, and Germany the point is always seized, because the average opera-goer in those countries is as familiar with *Don Giovanni* as the Englishman is with *Come into the garden, Maud.* Moreover, in Offenbach's score the phrase is given in Italian, the end being slightly altered from the original— "*Notte e giorno mal dormire*" instead of "*Notte e giorno faticar.*" In this country the line is always sung in English, for the Italian would be utterly incomprehensible to the monoglot British public. Thus do composers make musical jokes in vain, so far as the kingdom of Great Britain and Ireland is concerned!

It is a pity educated people do not know music as well as they do their own and foreign literatures, for then a whole new world of delightful allusion would be open to composers, and some rich effects could be made, especially for comedic purposes. The music hall, in its own limited way, is doing something of the kind. The music hall public is a fairly constant one, that keeps well abreast of whatever goes on in its own small sphere. It knows pretty well all the popular songs of the last few years, and the most delicate allusion to a phrase from one of them in the accompaniment to another is detected at once. Some quite good fun is made in this way. It does one good to observe how quick the house is to see the joke; and it makes one wish there was a similar community of musical culture in the concert room and the opera-house. But in this country, at any rate, the average man knows so little of music that a composer might fill his score with quotations from other composers' works without the audience detecting one of them—unless it was a well-known hymn. No doubt everyone recognizes the tune of " Sleepers, wake," when he hears it in Mendelssohn's *St Paul.* In *The Huguenots* Meyerbeer uses the melody of " A stronghold sure " (Luther's hymn " *Ein' feste Burg* "), to symbolize the Protestant faith. One would hardly imagine that the dullest of auditors could fail to perceive the allusion here; yet I remember one performance of *The Huguenots* at which the man sitting next to me started up in alarm when the overture began with "A stronghold sure"; he thought he had strayed into church by mistake, and it took me a minute or two to persuade him that he was really sober.

Beyond the recognition of this obvious sort of allusion in music I do not think it is possible for the British public to go. Probably not more than one-tenth of one per cent. of the ordinary audience would know that a phrase in one of Elgar's *Enigma* Variations is a quotation from Mendelssohn's *Calm Sea and Prosperous Voyage* overture, unless they were told so in the analytical programme. So little do they know even of their own contemporary great men that hardly one of them would notice the many quotations Elgar has made from himself in *The Music Makers*, or know their origin when they were pointed out to him. And of course, unless the hearer not only knows that a quotation *is* a quotation, but has some knowledge of the work in which the original appears, the whole point of the illusion is lost on him. He may be told that the "Childhood" theme in *Tod und Verklärung* is a quotation from Strauss's early opera *Guntram*; but unless he knows that opera the theme as he hears it in *Tod und Verklärung* cannot bring with it the peculiar atmosphere in which Strauss intended to bathe it. In the medley of quotations from his earlier works that Strauss has inserted in one section of *Ein Heldenleben*, as some of the phrases are used merely as counterpoints it does not greatly matter whether we know their source or not ; but one or two of them—such as the melody of the *Traum durch die Dämmerung*—are much more poignant when their source is known. I doubt whether it would be wise of a composer to rely on the most elementary know-ledge of the world's music on the part of the average Briton. In Dr Ethel Smyth's breezy comic opera, *The Boatswain's Mate*, the police-man knocks at the door of the inn to the accompaniment of the motive of *Fate knocking at the Door* from Beethoven's fifth symphony. Musicians, of course, would recognize so obvious an allusion as this at once ; but probably the only effect on the plain man who had heard the symphony now and then during the last ten years would be to make him wonder where the dickens he had heard that tune before. Even on the literary side he could not be expected to understand the irony of those portions of *Feuersnot* in which Strauss and his librettist scourge the people of Munich for their failure to see the greatness of Wagner when he lived among them, and the greatness of the later musician who was born among them ; while of course our simple Englishman would never know that a certain theme that is used with humorous effect at this point of the score is the "giants" motive from the *Rhinegold*. It is a dangerous thing joking with the average Briton ; for he has a way of taking irony in the theatre with deadly earnestness, and, on the assumption that the author is talking nonsense, he has a nasty way of walking out in order to show his superior mind. One trembles to think what would happen in an English theatre during the scene, in Goetz's delightful opera *The Taming of the Shrew*, in which Lucentio, disguised as a pedagogue, makes love to Bianca under cover of a lesson in Vergil. Imagine the British " gods " when Lucentio began with his " *Arma virumque cano, Trojae qui primus ab oris.*" They would probably ask the actor, as Mr Potash asks Lawyer Feldman when he talks in Latin tags, to address his remarks to them in English, not Swedish.

How many of our people, again, who have seen *Parsifal* at Bayreuth or elsewhere recognize that in the scene of the swan Wagner hints in the orchestra at the " swan " motive in *Lohengrin?* There is a delightful musical allusion, too, in the third act of *Die Meistersinger*, where Eva declares that if her choice were free she would ask Sachs to marry her, and the wise old cobbler declines, on the ground of the disparity between his age and hers. " My child," he says in effect, " I know the grievous tale of Tristan and Isolda, and I have no desire to play King Mark." The orchestra gives out here a motive from *Tristan* that ought to be familiar to every one who has heard even the prelude to that opera in the concert room; yet at no performance of *Die Meistersinger* in England have I observed anything in any spectator's face to indicate that he had caught the allusion. (The quotation from Mark's monologue he could not be expected to recognize unless he knew *Tristan* thoroughly.)

H

Perhaps the subtlest use ever made of musical quotation was by Hans von Bülow. Musicians will remember that in the finale of the Ninth Symphony, after the orchestra has put forward, as it were, all sorts of thematic suggestions, Beethoven introduces the choral portion by making the baritone say, "O friends, not these tones ; but let us sing something more full of gladness." Bülow once came on to play a pianoforte solo after a soprano with a hideous screeching voice had sung. Bülow quietly preludized on the theme: "O friends, not *these* tones . . . !" As the incident happened in St Louis, U.S.A., it is doubtful whether many in the audience saw the joke ; but what would its fate have been in the Birmingham Town Hall, or the Manchester Free Trade Hall?

SOME MUSICAL PARODIES

WRITING a little while ago on the subject of musical allusion—the use of quotation in a musical work, as one quotes in prose—I suggested that, given a public instructed enough, there was an illimitable field for fun in musical parody. At that time I was not aware that anything of this sort had ever been published, though musicians gathered together have often amused themselves with rough-and-ready improvisations of parody. Wagner, for instance, used to divert his guests with a piano performance of the *Tannhäuser* overture as some academic musician of the day would probably have harmonized it. That more has not been done in this way is due partly to the fact that the public as a whole does not know the styles of the different composers well enough to be able to recognize good parodies of them, and partly to the fact that it is only within the last generation or so that the vocabulary of music has become large enough, and the technique of composition varied enough, to permit of the manipulation of music in this style or that by some clever person who stands outside all styles yet sees into the secret of each of them. An excellent beginning, I find, has been made in some little pieces by Alfred Casella (one of the leading Italian composers) and Maurice Ravel, entitled *"A la manière de . . . ."* The first volume, containing parodies of Wagner, Fauré, Brahms, Debussy, Strauss, and Cèsar Franck, all by Casella, was published in 1911. The second volume appeared in 1914: it contains parodies of Borodin and Chabrier by Ravel, and of Vincent d'Indy and Ravel by Casella.

Not all the pieces are parodies in the strictest sense of the term. In the genuine parody, the humorist suggests his victims' mannerisms of thought and of phrase without actually using any of them. Mr Oliver Herford's delightful *Rubaiyat of a Persian Kitten*, for example, is not a true parody. It is an imitation, in which many of the well-known phrases of the original are simply given a new and comic turn, as in the line, " We come like kittens, and like cats we go." The best literary parodies in the English language, I suppose, are the immortal one of George Meredith by Max Beerbohm and those of our poets by Mr J. C. Squire in his recent volume, *Tricks of the Trade*. In the perfect parody, the artist plays the bowling all the time off his own bat, so to speak. That is to say, he does not merely embroider a familiar tissue with threads plucked from his victim's fabric. Mr Daniel Gregory Mason's *Yankee Doodle* in the style of several modern com- posers is thus not a true parody. We only get the real thing when the parodist suggests not merely the style of his original but his innermost way of thinking. The real parody must be so like the original that if we did not know from the title-page that it *was* a parody we might be completely taken in by it. Max Beerbohm's parody of Meredith fulfilled this condition in perfection. Mr Squire can generally do all he wants in the way of spoofing, but he loves a mischievous flourish now and then that lets everyone see he is spoofing. He is sometimes not content to impersonate his victim : when the performance is over he kicks the poor wretch out contemptuously. It is thus that he deals, for example, with Sir Rabindranath Tagore. His Swinburne is quite as good as a great deal of the real Swinburne. It is perhaps from this particular parody that we can best distil the essence of parody. Every artist, even the greatest, has unconscious *tics* of thought and of style. They represent his brain's way of taking the line of least resistance. If they are particularly pronounced and of particularly frequent use, they can be isolated and used by the parodist to create the illusion of the original voice and hand. But both voice *and* hand must be imitated ; not only mannerisms of style—such as Grieg's falling thirds, or Elgar's sequences and solidly-moving basses—but the subject's way of thinking.

Judged by this test, not all the Casella-Ravel parodies, good as they mostly are, come quite up to the level of our finest literary parodies. Sometimes Casella fails just where one would have thought the problem, for so excellent a musician, was easiest. Nothing in a man's style could be more strongly pronounced, for instance, than Franck's gliding chromaticism ; yet Casella does not reproduce it particularly well, and therefore, of course, gets nowhere near suggesting the real body of Franck's thought. In the cases of composers with very marked mannerisms or poses, parody of a sort becomes almost too easy. Thus Casella, in the *Almanzor, ou le Mariage d'Adelaïde*, has no difficulty in imitating the sort of sham cleverness with which Ravel occasionally imposes, if not on his hearers, at any rate on himself. The Debussy parody (*Entr'acte pour un drame en préparation*) is practically perfect; but then Debussy's mannerisms are so patent and used so woodenly that the imitation of him is almost too easy; it is like stealing a penny out of a blind man's tin. If this imitation suggests quotation rather than pure parody here and there, it is because Debussy himself is always quoting from himself, and a good many of his pages look like parodies of himself. Casella's Strauss (*Symphonia Molestica*) is first-rate. The parody, by the way, is obviously not of the *Symphonia domestica*, but of *Ein Heldenleben*; and the *tics* of style of that work are very cleverly seized upon—the impetuous melodic rushes, the sudden modulation out of the key and as suddenly into it again, the torrential scale passages, the emphatic repeated chords, like a succession of hammer-blows, at the top of a climax, the obvious melodic imitations in the inner parts, and so on. But some touches and phrases come too near actual quotation to be quite perfect parody. The modulation and the turn of melody in the opening bars of page 15, for instance, are obviously taken straight from the love section of *Ein Heldenleben.* Casella's parody of Fauré (*Romance sans paroles*) is extraordinarily clever ; so is Ravel's version of " Gentle flowers in the dew " (from *Faust*), as Chabrier would have written it. His imitation of Borodin does not strike me as quite so good. Casella is undoubtedly the real master at this sort of thing. His Vincent d'Indy (*Prélude à l'après-midi d'un Ascète*), with its heavy harmonies, its capricious rhythms, its coquettings with the whole-tone scale, and its truly d'Indyan mixture of styles, shows how sure an eye he has for his victim's foibles. The Brahms (*Intermezzo*), again, reproduces admirably some of the most pronounced of the Brahms mannerisms —the clumsy strength, mollified by occasional German-sentimental sixths, the cross rhythms, the alternative section in the folk-style, the growling basses, the thick harmonic colour, and so on. It is all so good that it might well be mistaken for Brahms. So again with the Wagner (*Einleitung des 3 Aufzuges*), which I think is the best parody of them all. It might really be taken by the unwary for a couple of pages of the Wagner of the *Götterdämmerung* period. This, surely, is the ultimate test.

MAD MONARCHS AND MUSIC

MONARCHS, as a rule, do not interest themselves in music except as an amusement for an idle hour. When they care for it a little more than this, the probability is that they are mad—to this degree or that. In the eighteenth century a king of Spain took Farinelli, the greatest Italian singer of his day, from the stage, loaded him with gifts, and made him his chief adviser in affairs of State. I have always doubted the sanity of that king, for no one except a lunatic or a woman would go crazy over a tenor (or the eighteenth-century equivalent of the tenor). Frederick the Great was very fond of music, patronized Bach and other composers, and played flute duets with Quantz. After this, one hardly needs to read Macaulay to learn that in many respects Frederick was intellectually and morally abnormal. The only monarch of the nineteenth century who did something vital for music was the mad King Ludwig of Bavaria, to whom, indeed, it is impossible for the world to exaggerate its indebtedness. But though Ludwig did so much for Wagner, it seems to be beyond dispute that it was the poet and prose writer rather than the great composer who commanded his admiration. It is doubtful whether the king was capable of appreciating *Tristan*; his favourite opera is said to have been *Il Trova-*

tore. It is depressing to consider, again, that in our own day the only European monarch who has shown a desire to shine in music—to say nothing of the other arts—is the Kaiser, some aspects of whose career really tempt one to believe in the theory of the transmigration of souls. A few years ago a daring German professor satirized the Kaiser very cleverly, and with perfect safety, in what purported to be a study of one of the Roman emperors. I forget which of the emperors seemed to him the reincarnation of the Kaiser; but I should say the nearest approach to him in the ancient world was Nero.

When a monarch falls a victim to artistic vanity he seems to get the disease very badly, for he is not subject, as the plain man is, to the healthy, honest criticism that is so good for all of us. Judging from his actions and his deliverances, it has never occurred to the Kaiser to doubt his own competence to decide any purely artistic question, from the value of Strauss's music—which he dislikes—to the authenticity of the pseudo-Leonardo bust. He commands painters and musicians to paint certain pictures and write certain operas, no doubt feeling all the time that he could do them much better himself if only he had the time. But so far as I know he has not yet ventured to appear in public as a musical performer; and that is where Nero was a long way ahead of him. Nero is indeed the most striking example of artistic megalomania among monarchs. He believed himself to be

the superior of every professional in every art.
Now and then his mania took a really good turn,
as when he insisted, like Ludwig, on the re-
building of certain parts of his capital in better
style. He thought himself not only an architect,
but a poet, a painter, a sculptor, an actor, and
a gladiator; but if he had been asked to name
the art in which he really excelled he would
have modestly whispered, " Music."

Apparently he believed he could play any
instrument, and he decidedly fancied himself as
a singer. He often took part in musical com-
petitions, and invariably carried off the first
prize. A cynic might suggest that the adjudi-
cators, if not particularly good judges of music,
were excellent judges of human nature, and had
a very fair idea of what would happen to them
if they preferred an ordinary man's singing to
the Emperor's. Nero himself had never any
doubt as to his own superiority. When Rome
was beginning to get seriously out of tune with
him as an emperor, nothing in the gibes of his
enemies wounded him so much as being called
"a pitiful harper." There is an American story
of a German orchestral musician who declared
himself to be the finest double-bass player in
New York. A rival heatedly challenged him
to prove it. " Dere is no need to prove it," said
the German; "I admit it." Even so did Nero
admit, to those who carried to him the remarks
current in Rome concerning him, that he was
without a rival in his special line. " Passing by
the other accusations as wholly groundless," says

Suetonius, "he earnestly refuted that of his want
of skill in an art upon which he had bestowed
so much pains, and in which he had arrived at
such perfection; asking frequently those about
him 'if they knew anyone who was a more
accomplished musician?'" The answer was
almost certainly in the negative; any other
would have been tactless, seeing that Nero had
put a certain Paris to death as a dangerous rival
(the analogy with the Kaiser becomes quite
close at this point), and, like the Kaiser again,
had tried to poison Britannicus "out of envy
because he had a sweeter voice." If the worst
came to the worst, he thought, he could earn his
living anywhere as a musician: as he put it,
"An artist could live in any country." This
consoling reflection was no doubt inspired by
the memory of his public triumphs as a singer,
especially during his tour in Greece. In Rome,
an impresario offered him a million of sesterces
if he would accept a professional engagement.
Like the modern singer, he had no great opinion
of the abilities of his rivals. "That no memory
or the least monument might remain of any
other victor in the sacred Grecian games, he
ordered all their statues and pictures to be pulled
down, dragged away with hooks, and thrown
into the common sewers." I believe modern
singers sometimes feel like that when they open
the paper the morning after a concert and find
the critic praising a colleague more than themselves. And just as the singer of to-day, while
professing a lordly contempt for criticism, spends

scores of pounds per annum in reprinting *favourable* criticisms of himself, so Nero had carried before him "inscriptions denoting the places where his prizes had been won, from whom, and in what plays or musical performances." Very like a modern singer with his criticisms, again, was Nero, when "he offered his friendship, or avowed open enmity, to many, according as they were lavish or sparing in giving him their applause." Human nature hardly changes throughout the ages, and musical human nature least of all.

But Nero had a great advantage over the modern singer in the fact that he was an absolute monarch. Apparently as sensitive to criticism as they are, he did what some of them have been known to do—engaged a claque to kindle enthusiasm in the audience. But Nero did the thing on a proper scale. He chose, says Suetonius, besides young men of the equestrian order, "above five thousand robust young fellows from the common people, on purpose to learn various kinds of applause, called *bombi* [the humming of bees], *imbrices* [the rattling of hail on the roof], and *testa* [the clattering of earthenware], which they were to practise in his favour whenever he performed." These gentlemen, we are told, "were remarkable for their fine heads of hair, and were extremely well dressed, with rings upon their left hands." One seems to have met people very like this in the musical and theatrical world, among the concert agents and press agents. The claque is a device open to any singer; but the moderns would give their ears to be able to play Nero's trump card. "During the time of his musical performance, no one was allowed to stir out of the theatre on any account, however necessary; insomuch that it is said that some women with child were delivered there. Many of the spectators being quite wearied with applauding him, because the town gates were shut, slipped privately over the walls, or, counterfeiting themselves dead, were carried out for their funeral." Other devices of his for gathering in the applause are not unknown to the musical world of to-day. "As if his adversaries had been on a level with himself, he would watch them narrowly, defame them privately, and sometimes, upon meeting them, rail at them in very scurrilous language; or bribe them, if they were better performers than himself." No modern singer, of course, would stoop to this last infamy, for the simple reason that a search with a lantern at mid-day would not enable him to find better performers than himself.

Nothing, to my mind, redounds more to the credit of Nero than his singing while Rome was burning (the "fiddling" of the popular phrase seems to be an error; as he watched the fires he himself had lighted he "sang a poem of the ruin of Troy"). It was the act of a true artist, who knows that life is never so real as art, and that in this world it is A's business to suffer while B enjoys himself making a poem or symphony out of A's suffering. To do Nero justice, when the time came for him to go the way of all tyrants, when he knew that death was near, either by his own hand or that of his enemies, he indulged in no sentimental reflections, as Marcus Aurelius might have done, upon the future of mankind in general. The cry of his heart was "Alas, alas! what an artist is now about to perish!" And at least he had the grace and the courage to cut his own throat when he realized that the world did not sufficiently appreciate an artist like himself. For some modern musicians who, as artists, have seen their best days, a worse fate is reserved; they linger on till they are knighted.

THE VILLAIN IN MUSIC

LISTENING again to *Otello* the other evening, and following with particular interest Verdi's delineation of Iago, I made up my mind that after the performance I would compare Iago with other villains of opera. When I began to do so, however, I found surprisingly little data for comparison. To my disappointment, operatic villains were exceedingly scarce; the manufacture of them seems to be one of the great neglected industries. Of the few villains one does find in this field, the majority reveal their villainy rather in their words than in their music; that is to say, from their music alone we could not size them up as villains. This fact in turn set me thinking. Music is obviously able to limn most characters for us almost as definitely as words or painting can. Long before I had seen *The Valkyrie* on the stage, I knew, simply from the theme that precedes Hunding's entry in the first scene, that Hunding was an ugly, hulking fellow with a big fist and a black beard. You can tell from Tristan's music that Tristan never smiled from his birth. Listen to ten bars of Parsifal's music, and you can see at once that Parsifal was no good at sports, and that, for all his talk about his martial adventures, when the time came to loose his snicker-snee on an opponent's abdomen he would have turned conscientious objector.

We know, from their music alone, not only that
Eva and Gutrune and Gretel and Mélisande are
nice girls, but that they are different types of
nice girls; and that while Gutrune would never
have attended a woman's suffrage meeting,
Brynhilde would certainly have been there, and
in the chair at that. In these and a hundred
other cases we can not only realize characters
from their music, but actually visualize them.
No tenor in the world will ever persuade me
that Tristan could put on flesh: the fever of
his nerves would never have permitted that.
A brunette Eva or a blonde Carmen is unthinkable; and the trouble with most performances of
Madame Butterfly is our feeling that the
prima donna weighs so much more than the
music tells us Butterfly ought to weigh. Beck-
messer's music tells us as plainly as words can
do that he has a slight hump, a slight crick in
the neck, and walks with a nervous fussiness:
one adder-like dart of Hagen's theme at us, and
we know there is not an ounce of superfluous
flesh on that grim, granitic body. All this, as I
say, we visualize from the music alone, before
we have seen certain operas on the stage; yet
the villains we can rarely visualize from their
music alone, even *after* we have seen them on
the stage.

Can it be true, after all, that Ruskin was right
when he said that the maiden can sing her lost
love, but the miser cannot sing his lost money
bags—that there is a limit to the expressive and
descriptive power of music, and that, precisely

because music is an affair of the heart, it becomes impotent when it is set to suggest the absence of heart? A man sings because he has an impulse to show himself as he is ; but in the terms of the case it does not suit a villain to show himself as he is. See, says the lover to the other people on the stage, how much I love, and how well I can express my love. See, says Elisabeth, how pure I am. See, says Elektra, how mad I am. See, says Hans Sachs, how wise I am. But the villain cannot come forward and say, " See how vile I am." And apart from this, there is surely something in the very nature of music that puts a gilding of beauty over the harshest things a character may say. It is like trying to look savage and smile at the same time. It may be, of course, that the resources of music will expand in this respect beyond anything we can at present imagine. A thousand things can be said in music to-day that could not have been said in the eighteenth century ; and it is possible that the psychological range and the expressive power of the musical dramatist of the future may as far exceed those of Wagner as those of Wagner exceed Mozart's. One remembers how Beethoven failed when he tried to reproduce the Goethe lyrics in music, and how Mozart's Figaro is as far in wit and agility of mind from Beaumarchais' Figaro as a merry schoolboy is from Voltaire. Perhaps when the resources of operatic music shall have become as much wider than those of Wagner as Wagner's are than those of Mozart we shall have the villain made as re-

I

cognizable in his music as the hero now is —and not merely the villain but the precise shade of his villainy. But at present the problem is rather beyond the powers of our dramatists.

There is, of course, a certain routine of villainous presentment in opera, but it is mostly only routine—a thing of orchestral tricks and dodges, hardly touching the springs of psychology more deeply than thunder-and-lightning effects, or the emotional dither in the strings when the dying hero of melodrama thinks of his mother. This is merely standardized villainy, good enough in its way, but at best only a machine-made article. A fair specimen of it is Wagner's Ortrud. Effective as she is, it must be admitted that we get our insight into her by way of her words rather than by way of her music; whereas a character like Elsa or Gutrune does not need to utter an intelligible word for everyone to be able to read her like a book, simply from the music she sings or the music the orchestra weaves round her. It is this general conventionalizing of the portrait of the villain that makes one wonder whether music has really a very wide scope of portraiture in this department of psychology. Scarpia is a thorough villain, but Puccini's music throws little light on any side of his character except the erotic, in which, needless to say, music is quite at home. After all, I imagine, there are only two really striking figures of villains in all opera—Iago and Hagen. Shakespeare's Iago is a *tour de force* :

in his frank declarations of his own turpitude he would come very near melodrama were it not for the superb instrument of language of which Shakespeare makes him the master. How has Verdi managed with Iago? It is evident that the character fascinated him, and that he has taken special pains with him. I lay no great store by the *Credo* of his own villainy that Boïto has put in his mouth; good as it is, it is only what I call the routine expression of operatic wickedness. A German would have done this better, one thinks; the Italian opera composers have never been very skilled in making music talk philosophy. Where Verdi's Iago is most vital is where he suggests what we are perhaps not wrong in regarding as typically Italian elements. This Iago is much more graceful, courteous, insinuating, and subtle in a serpent-like way than the Iago of Shakespeare. The latter's drinking song has nothing of the seductive rascality of the Italian Iago's. Verdi, in fact, has—apart from the *Credo*—skilfully selected and heightened just those aspects of such a character that music is most fitted to deal with. There is a peculiarly sinister quality in the quiet music that accompanies Iago's story to Othello of how he slept with Cassio; the music seems to have the velvet tread and the dangerous alert eye of a panther stalking its prey. Music, again, lends itself easily, by means of harmony, to the distilling of such poison as seems to exude from the tissue of Iago's "Oh! beware, my Lord, of jealousy." In his catechism of Othello—

" Did Michael Cassio, when you woo'd my lady,
   Know of your love?" etc.—

there is again something extraordinarily sinister
—a deadliness of insinuation that goes far beyond
anything that Shakespeare can suggest in words;
though it is unfortunate that Othello, in replying
to the queries, should speak so much as he does
in the idiom of Iago, Verdi being apparently
unable here to keep the dialogue within the
frame of musical form and yet differentiate the
two personalities.   Another example of a kind
of working that is peculiarly the property of
music is to be seen in the first scene of the
second act, where the orchestral figure that is
at first so smooth and cajoling becomes as brutal
as an oath and a blow as soon as the duped
Cassio has gone, and Iago, left alone, can let
fall his mask.   Yet though Verdi does so much
with Iago, what he does merely makes us the
more conscious of how much he has had to
leave undone.   Hagen is the more terrible
because Wagner does not so much depict him
as suggest him.   One touch of portraiture there
is, and it is a master-touch—those two notes,
falling an augmented fourth, that give a hint of
grimness that is beyond all parallel in music.
Wagner, with his infallible artistic insight, saw
that the surest way to suggest the horror of
Hagen was harmonically—by means of a harsh
interval that could be wrought into the tissue
of almost any bar.   The very terseness of the
characterization is in keeping with the cold,
gaunt strength of Hagen.   And by making the

characterization harmonic rather than melodic, Wagner not only evades successfully the problem —perhaps insoluble—of finding music for Hagen to sing that shall consciously express his villainy, as Verdi is always trying to do with Iago, but he confers on Hagen a terrifying omnipresence throughout a great part of the drama. When Verdi's Iago is not singing or not present we forget him. We are never allowed to forget Hagen even when he is not on the stage ; he is there in the spirit, harmonically, in the tissue of many and many a passage, like a poison working invisibly in a doomed body. So he becomes not merely a character but a cosmic force, a finger of fate, while Verdi's Iago is never more than so much flesh and blood in a stage costume. And it may be that this is the lesson for the musical dramatist—that it is more as a symbol than a character that the villain will always have to be treated if the full measure of his villainy is to be conveyed to us in music.

CRITICISM BY CODE

IN a recent article I referred to the diabolical custom inaugurated in Manchester by Mr Frank Merrick and his wife (Miss Hope Squire), of giving concerts without disclosing the names of the composers whose works are being played. I pointed out how unfair this was to the critics, who could not reasonably be expected to say whether a given piece of music was good or bad unless they knew whether it was by a Wagner or a Wilkins, a Beethoven or a Binks. Unmoved by my anguished protest, Mr Merrick goes on his cruel way. He sends me the programmes of two of these hunt-the-slipper concerts of his. I reprint them here, that the reader may see for himself how impossible the work of the critic will be made if everyone adopts Mr Merrick's plan :—

(1) Duet for two pianofortes, in three connected movements — namely, a Prelude, twenty-nine Variations on a Ground Bass, and a Fugue.

(2) Pianoforte Duet, in rondo form.

(3) Pianoforte concerto in one movement, of which a large section forms the central portion.

(1) Variations and Fugue on a Borrowed Theme, for two pianofortes.

(2) Sonata for two pianofortes, in three movements.

(3) Spanish Suite, arranged for two piano-

fortes from the orchestral score; (*a*) "Along the streets and alleys"; (*b*) "The perfumes of the night"; leading to (*c*) "The morning of a holiday."

In other words (I quote from memory),

> "They played him a sonata—let me see,
> Medulla oblongata, key of B ;
> Then they began to sing
> That extremely pretty thing,
> 'Scherzando ma non troppo, ppp.'"

The only thing for the critic to do if this infamous dodge becomes general, is either to wrap HIS contribution to the entertainment in such mystery that no one will be able to make out which side of the fence he is sitting on, or to take the bull by the horns and say boldly just what he thinks, and damn the consequences. I am assuming, of course, that he fails to "spot" the composers. It would not be easy to gravel him with the ordinary or even extraordinary concert repertoire, but the hardest student cannot be expected to know *everything* that is written for two pianos, or for violin or violoncello if he does not happen to play either of these instruments. If ever there was a provocative act, a diabolical plot, it is this. The only object it can have is to make us critics look even bigger fools than we are at present.

In Germany there has recently been formed a union of musical critics. The worm has turned at last. Tired of being trodden upon— or, which is worse, being sung at and played to

—he has combined with his fellow worms in an offensive (and we know how offensive critics can be) and defensive alliance against the common enemies of the species. I really must call a meeting of English musical critics some day, and see if we cannot draw up between us a sort of primer for the craft—a " When to Criticize, and How." The longer I am engaged in this nefarious business the more convinced am I that musical criticism occupies too much space in our newspapers. It is right to discuss a big work or a great performance as if it were something new and unique under the sun, which it undoubtedly is. But most compositions and most performances are so lacking in individuality that I am sure they could be "placed," in the critical sense, with far less expenditure of time and space and printers' ink than is wasted on them at present. It was only the other day, however, that I accidentally discovered, from a book that I shall mention shortly, the lines on which the musical criticism of the future will have to run. My own first idea was a system of marking, something like that in use at competition festivals. A vocalist or a fiddler might be given so many marks for tone, so many for intonation, so many for pace, rhythm, and accuracy, so many for enunciation, and so many for general intelligence (if any). Composers might be marked on the basis of (*a*) originality, (*b*) melodic interest, (*c*) harmonic interest, (*d*) rhythmic interest, and (*e*) technique. At the head of the critic's article would be set forth the manner and the scale of marking; and then the criticism would run something like this : —

New opera, " The Children of John," words and music by Lord Joseph de Walbrooke :

20 + 10 + 12 + 8 + 10 = 60 (out of a possible 100).

Aria, " *Una voce poco fa*," by Miss Ethel Howler :

10 + 5 + 8 + 7 + 0 = 30 (out of a possible 100).

But a book on Indian music by one Shahinda that has just come into my hands has shown me an even better plan than this—a system of code words. It was very stupid of me not to have thought of this before ; for, as most compositions and performances are very much alike, obviously a few code words could be made to indicate them all. What is the use of one critic saying that Mr Szplanowski's playing was good but his music was bad, and another that the music was bad but the playing was good, a third that the playing was better than the music, a fourth that the music was not so good as the playing, and so on and so on, when it could all be expressed in a single code word, just as a merchant cables, say, " Mahomet " to America, meaning thereby " Buy 20,000 Canadian Pacifics at not more than 190 "? Now the ingenious Hindoo mind, it seems, has already codified musical instruction in this way. According to Shahinda, each defect in singing is characterized by a single word. Thus " Sandasht " means " To sing with closed teeth " ; " Kanpat " means " To start with a tremor in the voice " ;

" Kagay " means " To start with commotion and noise "; " Karaba " means " To crane the neck like a camel "; " Abagpat " means " To sing with the words all jumbled up together, and rolling in the throat so as to be incomprehensible "; " Saanasik " means " To sing with a nasal twang "; " Kagay " means " That the voice should be like the crowing of a crow "; " Bhikan " means " That the voice should resemble the braying of a donkey." The vocal virtues are similarly codified. If the voice is " sweet and entertaining," that is " Mudhr "; if the voice is " possessed of such pathos as to produce deep feeling and tears," that is " Kaaran "; if the voice is " big and heard distinctly at a distance," that is " Sara-dak "; if " the command should be so entire as to be able to produce loud and soft at will," that is " Gaad "; if " the singer should be of a prepossessing appearance and noble disposition," that is " Parjar." How wonderfully simple it is, and yet how effective! I have once or twice experienced Parjar; occasionally it has been Mudhr or Kaaran; but times without number have I groaned under Abagpat, and fled in horror from Kagay and Bhikan. The system could easily be applied not only to singing and playing and composing, but to any event of the musical season; all we have to do is to agree upon a code word for each of the few contingencies that may arise. If a choral society, for example, gives *Hiawatha* for the heaven-knows-how-manyth time, the concert might be disposed of in the single word "Quakaa," which being decoded, would signify, "We have heard all this before. Have these good people been asleep for the last ten years?" and many other things. The beauty of this method is that it would be international. A man ignorant of German would pick up a German review to see what was thought of the latest work of Max Reger, and when he saw the word "Rajbaht" he would understand at once that "the music is extremely like all the other music of this prolific composer, his capacity for saying things being much in excess of his fund of things to say." I burn to go down to history as the man who codified musical criticism. I hereby summon my colleagues to a meeting on the 1st April next, at which, I hope, we shall lay the foundations of a new praxis.

A SYNDICATE OF MUSICAL CRITICS

THERE has recently been founded in Germany a league of musical critics, for the protection of the interests of the members of that profession. Some people will doubt whether a combination of this sort ought not to be declared illegal, as the combination of any other gang of enemies of the public peace would be. But from the critics' point of view the idea is certainly a good one, and I should like to see it put into operation in this country. It has always seemed to me that a musical critic is the worst business man on earth. He persists in stocking, against his own interests, an article which his chief customers have no desire to buy, and generally refuses to display the article for which the said customers would be willing to pay handsomely if they could get it. This may need some explanation. The chief customer of the musical critic is not the public, but the artist, under which term I include composers and performers of all kinds. The artists will tell you that they never read criticism, and hate and despise the whole community of critics. But don't believe them. They may not be interested in criticism in the abstract; but they read every word a critic says about *them*. I have heard an artist profess loudly that nothing that a critic could say would have the slightest weight with him ; and the next day I have seen half a column of the front advertising page of the *Daily Telegraph* radiant with the nice things the critics have said about him. So it appears that the artists despise only the criticism that looks down on them, and appreciate highly the criticism that looks up to them. Here, then, if the critic is wise, is a market worth developing. The critic who wants to get rich quickly should sell the praise that his customers are willing to buy. "Instead of which," as the country magistrate said to the man who stole the poultry, he regards it as a point of what he quixotically calls honour to say he doesn't think much of A or B when he honestly doesn't.

In America and on the Continent they manage things better. One great foreign musical paper derives a huge revenue from merely looking with a kindly eye on the artists who yearn for a little fellow feeling, and who, in quite a dis-interested way, are willing to present a specimen of their autograph (on one of the forms thought-fully provided by bankers for that purpose) to a journalist possessed of the kindly eye aforesaid. Owing to certain prejudices on the part of old-fashioned people, the journal refrains from announcing publicly that such-and-such a column about such-and-such a singer is a result of the friendly co-operation of the two parties. In Paris the system of sale and purchase is as a rule more open : consequently the opinions of the papers do not bring as much grist to the artist's mill as he has the right to expect from his expenditure.

It is some system of the former kind that I should like to see introduced into England, only —and this is most important—for the benefit of the critics, not that of the newspaper proprietors. As the critics supply the quo's, they obviously ought to get the quids. I do not think any musical critic objects as a matter of principle to being bribed—if I may be permitted to describe in the crude language of the vulgar what ought to be a very delicate and charming operation. I for my part certainly do not; all I expect is that the bribe shall be big enough to be worth taking. I have my price, like other men, and have no intention of lowering it. A whisky-and-soda or a cigar from a tenor, or a sweet look from a soprano, is not sufficient. If they will offer me as much as I might win in a football guessing competition—a motor-car, or £1000 a year for life, or a villa at Brighton—I shall consider it. After all, why be honest, as the cant phrase goes, when by a trifling relaxation of the moral tension you can not only benefit yourself, but give pleasure to a very large and deserving class of men and women?

But if a thing is worth doing at all it is worth doing thoroughly. The days of the individual trader are almost over: this is the day of the syndicate. I have once or twice suggested to my colleagues, when we have been gathered together at the autumn festivals, that we ought to syndicate musical criticism in England. My idea is for a comprehensive league of all the musical critics, with a central office somewhere— I would suggest Birmingham as being a very convenient place—with power to draw up a scientific tariff for every degree of praise, from the hint commendatory to the slobber hysterical, and for every class of artist, from the impecunious beginner to the Rothschilds of the profession ; and to see that no notice of any kind appeared in any paper until the artist had entered into friendly relations with the syndicate. We should outdo our benevolent friends of the Tariff Reform League ; we should not only make the foreigner pay—we should so broaden the basis of our operations as to enable every English artist to contribute according to his means and his necessity. A syndicate of this kind would be of infinite benefit to both artists and critics. The former would know precisely what to expect for what they had paid, and they would be sure of getting it. All obstacles to the free social intercourse of artists and critics would be removed. At present they do not mix freely, because the critic often does not care to make the acquaintance of a man whom it may be his unpleasant duty to disembowel the next day, while a delicately-minded artist avoids the critics for fear they should think he had interested motives for cultivating their society. All this shyness on both sides would be at an end. In the first place, the artist would deal direct with the central office of the syndicate, so that the individual critic in this town or that would have no more control over the nature or quality of the notice than an engine-driver has over the Board of Trade regulations for the running of railways; and in the second place, as there would be no notices but nice notices—for every wise artist would gladly place himself in the hands of the syndicate—there could no longer be any but the most friendly relations between artists and critics. The lion would at last lie down with the lamb, the cat with the mouse, the boa constrictor with the rabbit. And of course a syndicate of the kind I have suggested would raise the standard of music all over the country, for obviously there would no longer be any bad compositions or bad performances, at any rate by the clients of the syndicate. As the chief proprietor of the foreign journal to which I have referred used to say in his genially cynical way, "It's astonishing how a singer's voice improves after one advertisement in the ——."

The system would also lead to an improvement in musical criticism in certain places. My political readers have no doubt not yet forgotten the Mr Rosenbaum, or Rosenbloom, or some patriot with a similar good old English name, whom Mr Jeremiah MacVeagh discovered a little while ago and introduced to a delighted House of Commons. Mr Rosenbaum—let us call him that for short—ran a Central Intelligence Office for the supply of speeches on the Home Rule Bill for Unionist members of Parliament. I would have a Central Intelligence Bureau in connection with the Syndicate of English Musical

Critics, the business of which would be to tell the weaker brethren what to say when confronted with a work or person of whom they had never heard. Some unfortunate mistakes, calculated to let criticism down in the eyes of the scoffer, would thus be avoided in future. The classical case is that of the critic writing about the first performance of the Pathetic Symphony in his town ; not knowing anything about Tchaïkovski — not even that the poor fellow had been long since in his grave—he praised the work warmly but guardedly, patted the composer on the back, and told him that if he would only be a good boy, and kind to his mother, and keep off the drink—or words to that effect—he might some day write a very fine piece of music. These regrettable misunderstandings would be things of the sad dead past when my syndicate came into being. The more I think of the idea the more I like it.

K

MUSIC AND THE GROTESQUE

IN the first number of *Form* Mr Edmund J. Sullivan has an article on " The Grotesque " that is at once suggestive and disappointing ; it is admirable in its analysis of the essence of the grotesque, but stops short just at the point where we should have liked Mr Sullivan to carry the discussion on from the grotesque in nature to the grotesque in art. I am not sure that everyone will agree with him in linking the grotesque in art with demonology, and so indirectly with theology. That comes, I think, from regarding the grotesque too much from the point of view of the graphic arts alone. For these arts deal largely with man : and man grotesqued undoubtedly suggests the demonic and many things that seem a denial not only of the beautiful but of the good. It may be quite true that the cosmic process works incessantly towards not only goodness—which is the best possible ordering of thoughts and actions and desires—but also beauty, which is the best possible ordering of shapes and movements. All the same, there is the existence of evil to remind us that there may be some truth in the theory that God made only one half of the world, and the Devil the other half. And in the æsthetic sphere there are many things to suggest that the Devil has had a good deal to do with the making not only of souls but of bodies. It shakes our belief in the constant process of the world towards beauty when we see some of the ugly types upon which nature seems to have lavished as much labour as upon the bird of Paradise or the gazelle—types whose very persistence shows how well they chime with some chord at least in the scheme of things. I find it much easier to believe that a God made Dr Crippen than that a God made the pig or the hyena. The probability is that these and other monstrosities are the Devil's work. Mr Sullivan is most moved to loathing by the mandrill. " It is hard to imagine the planning of the mandrill," he says, "except by a malignant fiend, unless we are to agree with Pythagoras as to the transmigration of souls. . . . If we are God's tabernacles, surely the mandrill is the mansion of Beelzebub, from every window of which seven devils peer out. It would be impossible to invent a grotesque more awful in its intensity than this being . . . this poor beast, dowered apparently only with vice—Envy, Hatred, Malice and Lust—vice without satisfaction, nothing but satiety and discontent, a soul, in fact, in Hell . . . For us sinners he is an accusation, and a hint of what evolution along certain lines is capable of."

But even granting that the grotesque is of the Devil, we may still find a good and a philosophical word to say for it. The grotesque turned to hateful ugliness, as in the mandrill, is the Devil in convulsions ; but what of the Devil in his more thoughtful or more humorous moments—the Devil turned smiling critic of his fellow Demiurge? It is from this kindlier side of the Devil that a good deal of the grotesque of our artists comes; and only a pedant will deny that the Devil often makes out a good case for himself. After all, it is partly by luck that such-and-such types of fauna and flora have survived and not others; and some of those that have perished may have been handsomer than those that have survived. The animal and human grotesque is often a criticism of Providence—or at all events a polite suggestion. One of the fantastic drawings in *Form*, for instance, represents a being with six breasts. Providence has decided that the rule shall be two; but we can easily conceive of domestic circumstances in which six would be a decided improvement. And so with many another suggestion of the grotesque; if it comes from the Devil within, at all events it is from a very merry Devil, whose only crime is to believe that had he been consulted at the beginning he could have improved here and there on the world as we have it now.

Is the grotesque always to remain the special property of the pictorial arts? Architecture can obviously have few dealings with it; and the range of words on that side is limited. But one would have thought that music, with its unfettered lines, its endless combinations of colour, and its power of capricious rhythm, was an art peculiarly fitted for the cultivation of a grotesque of its own. It would needs be a subtler grotesque than that of drawing, because of the slightness of its connection with the material world.   The graphic arts recall to our eyes the shapes of daily life : it is because we all have a distinct mental image of the human body, for example, that we know the artist's flouting of this form to constitute the grotesque. Music, of course, cannot refer us in this way to the visible world at the same moment that it invites us to chuckle over its burlesque of it.   Yet there is plenty of music that manages very well, in spite of this limitation, to convey to us suggestions of the outer world; so that the non-material nature of music need not *a priori* be a bar to its dabbling in the grotesque. Most likely the explanation of the scarcity of the grotesque in music is the fact that the art is still in its infancy, still with a most imperfect knowledge of, and control over, its own resources. It was only yesterday, so to speak, that the orchestra became a really serviceable instrument for the suggestion of atmosphere and colour. When the possibilities of music are more fully realized, the Devil in man may have a better chance of kicking up his heels now and then. But there will always be one danger—that the Devil in music may become sanctified with the lapse of time, as has generally happened to him in the past.   For it is the peculiarity of music that its language is an incessantly growing one, as regards both vocabulary and grammar ; and it has a most pelican-like way of devouring its young.   The *Laocoon*   or   the   *Œdipus*

Rex is as passionate to-day as twenty centuries or more ago: but very little of the passionate music of even a hundred and fifty years ago has so much as a blush to its pallid cheek to-day. Growing as it is always doing in intensity and fullness of mere speech, music has a way of turning, in time, all its mightiest past to the primitive; no doubt the day will come when the hot red blood of *Tristan* will run as coolly and tranquilly as that of an Elizabethan love-song. It is by way of harmony that composers have hitherto mostly experimented, not so much with the grotesque as with the unexpected, that is after all the basis of the grotesque. Now time has rather a drastic way of dealing with novelties in harmony. If the harmony obviously does not talk sense, music in a very little time will reject it. If it *does* talk sense, then the art blandly incorporates it into its own being, makes a normal thing of it, breeds other harmonies from it, and so in time deprives it of that very element of unexpectedness that was the first justification of its birth. Take a modern instance that has already become classical. In *Don Quixote*, Strauss, as we know from the German programme annotators to whom he confided his intentions, employed a certain sequence of harmonies to suggest, by its paradoxical modulations, the Don's wrong-headed way of looking at things. But in a dozen years or so all the paradox has gone out of the harmonies: they seem as straightforward and natural now as any dominant-tonic cadence; and the result is that they make the Don appear not a wrong-headed gentleman, but a very respectable and indeed rather academic thinker.

Yet, digging our way through an obscure subject with the aid of such poor lamps as we have at present, we can see that it is not every stroke of unexpectedness in music that loses its virtue in the course of time. Some day a psychologist ought to give us a study of " The Element of Surprise in Art." On the surface of the case, no surprise ought to surprise us more than once. Some do not: at no later reading of *Vanity Fair*, for instance, do we again get the same shock and thrill as at our first reading of the end of chapter xxxii. : "and Amelia was praying for George, who was lying on his face dead, with a bullet through his heart." On the other hand no number of readings of *Œdipus* can diminish the horror of the *dénouement*; and at the fiftieth performance of *Die Götterdämmerung* our flesh creeps as grislily at the entrance of Siegfried in the guise of Gunther as it did at the first. Half of the effect of Hugo Wolf's wonderful *Denk' es, o Seele* comes from certain unexpected shiftings of the key: the effect, after a hundred hearings, is still one of unexpectedness. Plainly the thing *can* be done in music, though what the secret of it is, why it succeeds in one case and fails in another, we do not know. But since it *is* possible, we may reasonably hope that when the master of musical paradox comes—say in another hundred years—he will have at his service a harmonic and rhythmic instrument that will not break in his hands. And when music can find an expression that shall durably suggest both the thing guyed and the guying of it, the norm and the aberration, then the day of the true grotesque in music will have come; and then the merry mocking Devil in man will have a Walpurgis Night in comparison with which the hilarity of the draughtsmen will be only the decorum of a Sunday-school treat.

THE PERENNIAL BOHEMIAN

A PERFORMANCE of Puccini's *La Bohême* a couple of weeks ago sent me back to a re-reading of Murger's delightful and immortal book. I had not looked at it for a dozen years or more; reading it again now, I was struck by the closeness of the parallel between the literary and artistic life of Paris as Murger describes it in the 'forties and the musical life of the last decade or so that has centred in Paris. No doubt the conditions then were very much what they are now, allowing for changes in the aspect of things. Then, as now, the keen wit of Paris had slightly overrun itself. Artists with quite adequate reasons for not believing wholeheartedly in themselves found a consolation in mocking at the beliefs of others. Irony turned its acid stream upon sentiment then as now. Even in those days the blonde German art was a subject for the malicious laughter of the brighter Paris wits. A few years ago Romain Rolland's mordant satire of the sentimentality of German music—"the appalling German tearfulness"—made a number of good souls in all countries feel that a rude man was snapping his fingers in the face of our dear old maiden aunt and causing some commotion among the old lady's ringlets. But in the eighteen-forties Murger's Marcel was laughing as heartily as Jean-Christophe could have done at the "Teutonically sentimental tirades" of Rudolphe. The attempts of Scriabine and others to confuse the borders of sound and colour are no new thing: they are at least as old as the eighteenth century, and Schaunard seems to have been as mad after this hybrid, infertile mule-art as any modern of them all. His great symphony, *The Influence of Blue in the Arts*, would have been an excellent joke on Murger's part, and an anticipatory summary of many of the half-serious, half-ironic titles of to-day. But it was no joke on Murger's part. Schaunard was no creation of his own, but a study of his friend Alexandre Schanne, who lived on to 1887 and published his reminiscences of the Murger circle under the title of *Souvenirs de Schaunard*. This Schanne really wrote a symphony to which he gave the title of *The Influence of Blue in the Arts*. Like many another masterpiece, it was consistently refused by shortsighted publishers; but Schanne used to play the work to his friends, expounding it as he went along. He was as much painter as musician —how much or how little of each we have no means of knowing now; and his mind had become obsessed with blue as a result of painting from the top of the towers of Notre Dame. He no doubt lives on to-day in a reincarnation bearing the name of Erik Satie.

Had Satie lived eighty years ago, it would have been he who would have written Schaunard's symphony. It is Schaunard who to-day finds the titles for Satie's works—*Descriptions automatiques, Embryons desséchés, Gnossiennes, Heures*

*séculaires et instantanées, Peccadilles importunes,
Vieux séquins et vieilles cuirasses, Aperçus
désagréables, En habit de cheval, Trois Morceaux
en forme de poire,* and all the rest of them. The
more it changes the more it's the same thing!
Read Murger's preface to the *Scènes de la Vie de
Bohême* and see how phrase after phrase of his
description of the seething, inchoate mass of new
ideas in the literature and art of the Paris of his
own youth applies to the music of the too-con-
scious seekers after novelty in our day. The
Bohemians, he says, "speak amongst themselves
a special language." "All the eclecticisms of
style are met with in this unheard-of idiom, in
which [Erik Satie please note] apocalyptic
phrases jostle cock-and-bull stories, in which the
rusticity of a popular saying is wedded to
extravagant periods from the same mould in
which Cyrano de Bergerac cast his tirades; in
which paradox, that spoilt child of modern literature, treats reason as the pantaloon is treated in
a pantomime. . . . The Bohemian vocabulary is
the hell of rhetoric and the paradise of neologism."

Rhetoric in music, and especially German
rhetoric, is once more being consigned to hell;
and neologism in music is enjoying once again a
brief hour or two of paradise. Well, above the
ineffective literary Bohemianism of the Paris of
the 'forties there soared, in due time, the genius
of Hugo, of Balzac, of Flaubert—minds that
could fill rhetoric and sentiment with a fresh
spirit and that had too many really new things
to say to have any time for neologisms. Some-

thing of this kind, no doubt, will happen in music: irony, self-consciousness, and artistic vagabondage will exhaust their interest once more for a time, and a big, serious mind or two will express our own changed world to us as completely as the big men of the past expressed theirs. But the expression, I am quite sure, will not be in terms of neologism for neologism's sake. Gounod was no doubt right when he said that the next great composer would be great in virtue of his simplicity. By this we do not mean to-day a self-conscious simplicity, after the fashion of Strauss's recent coquetting with Mozartisms. The affectation of the unaffected is as tiresome as affectation for the sake of affectation. There can be no going "back to Mozart" or to anyone else. The new simplicity will be a modern simplicity, in which all the complexities of the modern soul will find expression, but in which this expression will be, like all the pregnant simplicities of art, a distillation of essence and a concentration of force.

The next great man will use not more, but fewer, notes than the average of to-day. We see the beginning of the process in Stravinsky, whose music, because he sees quite clearly what he wants to say and knows exactly how to say it, is really of an extraordinary simplicity of texture. But the coming great man will be less of a pictorialist and more of a humanist than Stravinsky; and when he is thoroughly master of himself and his medium his music will undergo just the same simplification as the music of

Beethoven, Wagner, and Wolf did in their last days.   It would not be surprising if the score of the future showed a delicacy of tissue that to Mozart himself would seem almost thinness.

Is it incredible that the next stage—or at any rate some future stage—of evolution should show us an implied rather than a stated harmony? Mr Huneker once amused himself by writing a story of a tympani enthusiast who wrote a long work for the drums alone.   It is quite possible that mere rhythm may have all sorts of meanings for us that we have not yet been able to evoke. But of the expressive power of pure melody— melody unaided by any harmony whatever—we become more conscious each decade.   The first great revelation of the suggestive force of such melody was the unison theme of the finale of the Ninth Symphony as it is first given out by the 'cellos and basses.   Wagner gave us further hints of the enormous latent force that is here awaiting development in the shepherd boy's *cor anglais* melody in *Tristan* and in the opening unaccompanied theme of the *Parsifal* prelude. Is it not conceivable that in time quite a long work shall be built up out of melody alone— melody so beautiful, so meaningful, that it shall seem to carry all the immensities along with it, that shall glide and bend with a more perfect suppleness because of its emancipation from harmony, but that shall still, like the *Tristan* and *Parsifal* melodies I have just mentioned, suggest all the eloquence and colour of harmony? The moving power of a beautiful glance depends on the mechanism and the chemistry of the eye, but the mechanism and the chemistry are kept by nature in the background. May not melody some day move us in the same way without the visible display of the harmony that colours and sustains it? But of melody of this kind only the greatest minds will be capable; it was not given even to Beethoven and Wagner to have more than a fleeting vision of it.

THE CONFESSIONS OF A MUSI-CAL CRITIC, IN AN OPEN LETTER TO A YOUNGER AND MORE INNOCENT MEMBER OF THE CRAFT

MY DEAR JOSEPH,—I have received with mixed feelings your letter telling me that you have been appointed musical critic to the *Manchingham Gazette*. I have the greatest liking and respect for you as a human being, but I doubt whether you possess the proper qualifications for a musical critic. As any "artiste" will tell you, a musical critic is not a human being, or, if he is, he is one afflicted with a bad form of homicidal mania. Are you sure you have the unnatural gifts and the immoral courage to enable you to live up to the ideal of infamy that will be expected of you from the moment you become a critic? On one point, at any rate, you may reassure yourself. The profession of musical critic is the easiest in the world. It is perhaps the only profession that can be practised by the man in the street with as much assurance as by the man who has given his life to it. It is a well-known fact that while no musical critic who ever lived is competent to argue about electricity with the electrician, or about surgery with the surgeon, not only the electrician and the surgeon but the butcher, the baker, and the candlestick-maker are all more competent to speak authoritatively on music than the critic. This fact is of itself sufficient to show you how easy it is to be a musical critic, and why it is that the profession attracts merely the intellectual derelicts of the human race.

However, once you have realized that you are a mere fool in music compared with the man in the audience who does not know the difference between Schubert and Schumann, or whether the saxophone is played with a bow or a plectrum, the profession has its compensations, and if you don't take it too seriously you may get a lot of fun out of it. But first of all let me implore you, Joseph, to adopt an attitude of becoming humility towards those great men and women who condescend to illuminate the world with their compositions, their singing, or their playing. You must surely see for yourself, if you reflect for only a moment, that it takes infinitely more brains to put a few black blobs on ruled paper, or to sing a scale fairly well in tune, or to play a pianoforte piece that millions of people have played before, than it does to run a millinery business in three capitals, or to drive a railway train through a thick fog, or to hold in private one set of political principles and expound in public another. Whatever you do, order yourself lowly and reverently towards these great persons in music, the least of whom is plainly your better. Your casual observation of them, on the platform or the stage, may cause you to form erroneous judgments as to the intellectual capacity of some of them, or to generalize too hastily about them in the mass. A long experience of singers, for example, may lead you to believe you can formulate a sort of natural law that the higher the voice the lower the intelligence. Don't think these blasphemous things, Joseph, or if you do, don't say them; pits have opened and swallowed malefactors up for less dreadful things than this. And remember that if you are duly humble and admiring you may even be admitted into the sacred presence of these masterpieces of creation. I do not hold out any hope that you will be as fortunate as myself, for I have been offered a cigar by a popular tenor, and have even had my hand pressed furtively by a comely contralto; but lesser favours, proportioned to your worth, will doubtless come your way in time.

But you will be unworthy even of the vile name of critic, my dear boy, unless your cunning finds some means by which to gratify with safety those malevolent instincts with which Providence has seen fit to curse the whole race of critics. It being an established medical fact that, while other men speak according to their lights, a musical critic always speaks according to his liver, you will do everything in your power to ruin your liver, consistently, of course, with remaining healthy and cheerful in the interval between your critical duties. But though your liver may degenerate to the extent of making you an absolutely ideal critic, you must always

L

keep your head cool enough to avoid that stupid British institution, an action for literary libel. Never forget that you are dealing with musicians —that is to say, beings so sacred that even to hint that each of them is not perfect in his own line is to commit something worse than the sin against the Holy Ghost. One politician may tell another that he has no honour, or accuse an opponent of frigid and calculating lying; a reviewer may tear a stupid and in- accurate book to pieces; but what are mere politicians and authors compared with top-note tenors and gramophone sopranos? If Mr Asquith were to bring an action against Mr Bonar Law for slander, or Mr Lloyd George were to try to have the law of Mr A. G. Gardiner, the public would wag its head and shoot out its tongue in derision. But the great men and women of the concert-room and the theatre are of a different clay. Therefore, my dear Joseph, handle them very carefully. Remember that you can say anything in the world, without fear of a libel action, if only you know how to say it. The knowledge that many of your criticisms will be gone over with a microscope in a lawyer's office will give you all the greater joy—the joy of the fox who has had a jolly day's exercise at the expense of the panting hounds and the hungry hunters, and enjoys a pleasant night's rest at the end of it all. Cultivate, therefore, my dear Joseph,

> The delicate and gentle art
> Of saying what you like.

The bulk of your work, of course, will be done at a late hour of the night, and I am afraid you will never be quite satisfied with it, for you will find that your ideas have a curious habit of getting lost between the concert-room and the office, and turning up again only on your way home. Still, as I have said, you can get a lot of fun out of the business if you go the right way about it. If you are saddened, as you are going home, by the recollection of the things you should have said but didn't, console yourself with a chuckle over the things you shouldn't have said but did.

I could give you heaps of other advice, but I will say no more now except this—and this is the most important thing of all. Wherever you are, make it your one object in life to ruin concerts and concert-givers. Everybody knows that musical critics hate music: and you will be no true critic if after, say, five or six years in a town there is any music left to criticize. Here again I can hold out no hope that you will be able to rise to my own heights of wickedness, though I trust you will do your best to reach the ideal. The means, you ask? The means, my dear boy, are extremely simple. All you have to do is to hint that composer A is not necessarily as good as composer B, or conductor C not as good as conductor D, and all the admirers of A and C will at once discover that it is impossible for A and C to go on living under infamous and venomous attacks of this kind. The public, who will of course take everything you say for gospel truth, will stay away in large numbers from concerts conducted by C, or at which the music of A is performed; and thus the glory of the red ruin that ensues will be all your own. Do not fear, however, that by *praising* A or C for some good thing they may chance to do you will be sending people to the concerts, and thereby defeating your object—which is to achieve the ruin of music in your town. The public, you will find, is really most sensitive and discriminating: it seems to know instinctively what you want, and while it will boycott anything you don't think much of, it will never go near something that you greatly admire. You are therefore perfectly safe. Do your worst then, Joseph, and may it be bad enough to bring joy to the heart of— Yours always, E. N.

A SECOND OPEN LETTER TO A
YOUNG MUSICAL CRITIC, ON
THE SUBJECT OF ENEMIES

M Y DEAR JOSEPH,—You have now been
the Musical Critic of the *Manchingham
Gazette* for something like eighteen
months, and you write me—with tears in your
eyes, I know—that everybody in the town seems
to dislike you. Foolish youth, what did you
expect from the public and the artists when you
became a musical critic? Love at first sight?
Did I not warn you, before you embarked on
this nefarious career, that in a few months you
would not have a friend left? I can never think
of a musical critic without being reminded of
Oscar Wilde's *mot* upon a certain English
dramatist. Someone asked Wilde if he knew
this gentleman. "Oh! I know him well," said
Oscar. "He's an excellent fellow. I don't
suppose he has an enemy in the world—but
his friends don't like him." The trouble with
the musical critic is that while his friends don't
like him his enemies positively detest him. It
was with this in my mind that I advised you,
if you felt hurt at what you would regard as
the injustice of the public towards you, simply
to grow a thicker skin and develop your sense
of humour. And here you are now crying like
a baby because one of your oldest friends has

turned against you, simply because you happened to say in your notice, as you were bound in common honesty to do, after you had heard him sing the *Pagliacci* aria, that you had heard Caruso sing it. You say if you go on like this you will not have a friend left in two years. Of course you won't; but why worry? Are you still so flabby of soul that friends are necessary to you? After all, what are friends? Mere luxuries. And do not the moralists tell us that the sign of a really strong spirit is the ability to deny oneself luxuries? I suppose you would have no hesitation in giving up smoking if the doctor told you it was bad for your heart, or wine if the doctor told you it was bad for your liver? Why then should you hesitate to give up friends if you realize that they are bad for your conscience? Self-indulgent coward! If thine eye offend thee, pluck it out; if thy friend offend thee, chuck him out. This simple rule of life, that is useful even for the plain man, is a vital necessity to the musical critic. Whatever mistakes you may make as a critic—and you are bound to make a few—never make the mistake of debasing your critical standards for a friend. If this is to be an egoist, then be an egoist. After all, what is altruism but doing unto others as they would never dream of doing unto you? When Huckleberry Finn had it explained to him that altruism meant sacrificing yourself for others, he remarked that that was awfully fine—for the others. You will discover that your composing and playing and singing friends will all want *you* to be the altruist, while they want to be—the others. But you will get over your first grief at this and all that it brings with it.   In time you will come to date your real happiness, the moment when you really began to live, from the day you lost your last friend through seeing him as he really is.   After that you will be free to think of him with affection and without embarrassment as you gaze at his photograph on your desk, and muse on the days that are no more. (Perhaps, however, you share with me a fondness for death masks?   I greatly prefer them to photographs; they are so much more lifelike.   Some day I hope to have death masks of all my old friends.)

But really, my dear boy, the public and the profession are very absurd over this question of friendship and criticism.   Here you are, as you say, raked by two fires; on the one side you have your friends giving you black looks because you try to judge them as impartially as if you had never known them; and on the other side you have the public firmly convinced—and even sending you anonymous and other letters to tell you of it—that whenever you praise or damn a man it is because you are a personal friend or enemy of his.   You know, of course, as well as I do, how foolish this is.   No one could ever tell from a critic's writing who were the people he personally liked and who the people he personally disliked.   Some of the best work I come across is done by men and women for whom, as men and women, I have almost an abhorrence ; while some of the people I like best cannot write or sing or play two bars without my wishing they wouldn't. But, as I have pointed out to you before, you are up against two remarkably strong forces in human nature. There is the vanity of the musician, who resents all criticism of himself, and cannot imagine how you can like So-and-so's work better than his unless you are a friend of So-and-so ; and there is the public, that also has its preferences and its prejudices, and, angered at seeing the critic smile at something it has applauded, quite naturally assumes him to be either a fool or a knave, or both. These good people never know how prone the critic is to over-praise a good thing for its own sake, or the anguish he has to endure when, for some reason or other, humanity forbids his saying how bad a bad thing really is. The other night, for example, I heard some Belgian opera singers —refugees—at a concert in aid of the Red Cross Fund. Never till then had I realized the horrors of war, the desperate plight of those poor Belgians who had to leave everything behind them in their flight from the Hun. These poor fellows had brought nothing away with them—not even their voices. And I sat there like a Christian martyr, smiling under my sufferings, resolved to die rather than show what I felt. We critics never get any credit for these things, Joseph ; but surely some day, in a better world than this, they will be counted

unto us for righteousness.   My own sole consolation is a belief in the transmigration of
souls—a belief that I recommend to you and all
musical critics as a never-failing source of
comfort.   I suppose in some previous existence
I must have been a bad dog, so in this life
the eternal powers made me a musical critic.
I have hopes that for my sufferings in that
capacity my next incarnation will be that of a
Pomeranian on some kind hearth.

And yet, my dear Joseph, and yet—for all
they say about you they won't be able to refrain
from reading you.   That is the amusing part of
it.   It is a surprising fact that the less you
worry about your enemies the more they worry
about you—another illustration of the adage
that while the saint is intensely interested in the
doings of the sinner, the sinner is not in the
least interested in the doings of the saint.   I
have just had an amusing illustration of this.
At a recent meeting of musicians, I am told,
no less a person than an archdeacon—think of
it, Joseph, an archdeacon!—made some disparaging remarks about *me*.   Even to be
disparaged by an archdeacon is an honour;
it shows that the intellectual highest in the land
are not indifferent to you, even if it is
only to dislike you.   This particular archdeacon
objected to what he called my dogmatism.
Yes, Joseph, I know what you are going to
say, that you can't understand a clergyman
objecting to dogma, that being, really speaking,
his own line of business.   But there is dogma

and dogma—the old, old story, you know, of orthodoxy or my doxy, and heterodoxy or thy doxy. Well, anyhow, however right or wrong the archdeacon may have been is not the point. There are really two points. The first is that archdeacons, who are men of great culture and discernment, voluntarily read musical criticism, whereas I search the pages of history in vain for any record of a musical critic who voluntarily listened to archdeacons' sermons; (it may be, of course, that archdeacons have a surer sense of what is good for them than musical critics have). The second point is that people, as you see, will read you, even if it is only for the luxury of disagreeing with you. So don't worry, Joseph, and don't take your enemies more seriously than they deserve. There is a lot of fun to be had out of them if you only go the right way about it,—Yours always,   E.N.

A THIRD OPEN LETTER TO A YOUNG MUSICAL CRITIC, ON THE SUBJECT OF LIBEL

MY DEAR JOSEPH,—Your letter distresses me beyond words. To be threatened with a libel action at this early stage of your career must indeed be disturbing. My poor lamb, my Iphigenia at Aulis, my Jephthah's daughter! Are the butchers at your quivering throat already? And all for what? Merely, as I understand, for saying that Claribel Cutt, whom you heard for the first time the other day, is not equal to her reputation. Of course she isn't; no musical performer *is* as good as his reputation, just as no musical critic is as bad as his. The horrible thing is that although nearly everybody will agree with you, nearly everybody, if he were on the jury that had to try your case, would give a verdict against you. As I have already told you, politicians and literary men may call each other liars, fools and humbugs, and neither they nor the general public will turn a hair. But to say a word against a composer or a performer is, in the eyes of the average juryman, a shade worse than the sin against the Holy Ghost. The law of libel is a very ticklish thing everywhere. I often think, with mingled sadness and amusement, of the case of Dr Leopold Schmidt, the musical critic of the *Berliner Tageblatt*. A

few years ago he wrote a very disparaging notice
of a German work that had been extensively and
expensively advertised. The publishers took
phrases here and there from his article, and by
cunningly joining them together converted it into
one of warm commendation. Dr Schmidt, in his
righteous indignation at this piece of sharp practice, wrote another article in the *Tageblatt*, telling
the publishers precisely what he thought of them.
Thereupon *they* brought an action against *him*
for defamation, and actually obtained substantial
damages—presumably from a jury composed of
relations of the cobbler of Koepenick. Let this
be a warning to you to steer clear of the British
law of libel, either as prosecutor or defendant.

Yes, yes, my dear boy, I know what you are
going to say—that your intentions are always
honourable, that you have no personal prejudice
against anyone, and that when you damn anybody
or anything it is solely in the sacred interests of
art. Your difficulty is to convince your victims
of that. Of course you and I know that feelings
of prudence or of humanity generally restrain a
critic from saying how bad a bad thing really is.
We are out to kill, but we don't want to hurt
anybody's feelings. How often, when I listen to
some screeching prima donna or some wretched
piano-strafer, do I feel inclined to cry out, as
Mr Perlmutter did to his partner, "If I would
say all that was in my mind, I could be arrested."
The performer and the public would no doubt
reply eagerly with Mr Potash, "Then hurry up
and say it, and get arrested." But that, my dear

Joseph, is where the cunning of the beast comes in. Your business as a critic is to convey all that is in your mind without being arrested. *Convey* it, you will observe, not say it. Make the reader an accomplice in your guilt; express yourself in such a way that he, not you, will supply the missing word that will just turn the laugh against your natural enemy the composer or performer. Did I ever tell you the classical story of the clown in the Berlin circus? It's too long to give you here point by point; but the gist of it is this, that some patter of his about the three Kaisers he had known led up to a mocking characterization of the present Emperor. The police warned him that if he said it again he would be arrested—which threat the management wisely allowed to become known, to the great benefit of the box-office on the following evening. The policemen were on the stage ready to do their duty. The clown went through all his patter as usual, and in time came to the very verge of the climax of the joke; but instead of himself applying the jibe to the Kaiser he asked the audience what *they* would call that potentate. They roared back the familiar joke in delight; the clown bowed and left the stage, and the policemen, looking very foolish, followed.

Now, my son, that is one of the lines of strategy you must develop. I shall write a book on this subject one of these days—" When to Libel, and How "; but for the present take one or two leading principles to go upon. Let me show you what I mean by the strategy of letting your readers themselves give the knockout blow. Suppose you were criticizing a beauty show, and the foolish public had awarded the first prize to a lady who was obviously, to an eye skilled in these matters, as ugly as virtue. If you were to say openly in your next day's article that the lady's husband was no doubt in the oculist's hands when he married her, you would lay yourself and your editor open to dire penalties. But you could convey the same idea much more effectively by simply quoting Dr Faustus' lines when Helen of Troy is brought before him—

> " Was this the face that launched a thousand ships,
> And burnt the topless towers of Ilium ? "

The lady herself, unread in literature and impervious to irony, would take it as a compliment; while the lettered public would see the joke and grin, and you would have the satisfaction of having got one home without any danger to yourself. Or suppose you have to deal with an obviously conceited young jackanapes of a composer Don't tell him, in so many words, that he is a featherbrained donkey ; just say, quite gravely, and with the air of paying him a respectful compliment, that he is the antithesis of Lord Goring. By the time he has tracked the allusion down to one of Oscar Wilde's plays, and discovered that Lord Goring was very clever but didn't like to be thought so, the Statute of Limitations will have come into operation, and you will be safe. When I begin my class for musical critics, the students will have to write exercises of this kind with perfect ease before a diploma will be granted them. You see already, however, the general idea, don't you? Be so slippery that no law and no lawyer could hold you for a minute. Suppose, to take another instance, that a thoroughly spoiled prima donna has sung a coloratura aria in a way that she thinks incomparable. Don't say a word in disparagement of her; simply express your contempt for the aria, and say that this sort of thing is only tolerable when done superlatively well. You can see with half an eye that if she were to try to bring your crime home to you it is on *her* that the burden of proof would fall; she would have to prove, to the satisfaction of judge and jury, that she *did* sing so superlatively well as to make this bad music tolerable to one who disliked it.

Of course irony never made any man beloved, and you must look forward to a large increase in the number of your enemies. But enemies, to a healthy-minded critic, are as tonic as a cold bath, and friends and admirers as relaxing as a hot one. It grieves you, Joseph, I know, to find that you already have so many enemies. You certainly do seem to be overdoing it a bit for one so young; here have I been in this business for about ten years, and I have only one enemy in the world—the public. But you must take your enemies as a huge joke. I myself know no more subtly delicious sensation than sitting in a hall full of people who dislike you. When English musical life becomes normal again, you will go the round of the provincial festivals.

There, my dear boy, you will drink to the dregs the sweet cup of enmity. The peculiarity of the festivals is this, that the hotel you are staying in is full of singers and composers and what not and their partisans; so that at breakfast each day you have the opportunity, denied to you under ordinary circumstances, of watching these dear people's faces as they read your articles, and catching the very glare of their eyes as they look up at you. Often and often, dear boy, have I made my cold coffee last out long after breakfast so as not to miss any of this comedy—to hear the prayer going up from many an agitated breast, "Gawd strafe Ernest Newman." In a way it's a compliment, as Smee says to the pirate captain in *Peter Pan*; it indicates a belief that with a criminal of your capacity no mere earthly tribunal is competent to deal. You, Joseph, will be no true pupil of mine unless at least once each day someone implores Providence to exterminate you. Get hated, my son, all you can; and to that end cultivate irony in its most insulting forms. My blessings on you.—Yours always,

E. N.

A FOURTH OPEN LETTER TO A YOUNG MUSICAL CRITIC, ON THE ART OF BLUFF

MY DEAR JOSEPH,—How often am I to tell you not to be alarmed at anything that may happen? Your position as a critic is of course full of difficulties; but there was never a difficulty yet from which an ingenious mind could not extricate itself with credit and even with glory. This last shock, though, I admit, is a serious one. I had already seen the American cuttings you sent me, in which it is suggested that the New York musical critics should be made to undergo an examination with a view to testing their capacity to sit in judgment on music and musicians. The proposed examination paper was a terror; a cold shudder ran through even a wily old hand like myself when I read it. It is obviously the work of my friend Mr Leonard Liebling, of the *New York Musical Courier*, a young man with an incurable passion for getting the utmost possible fun out of life. Mr Liebling, being a musical critic himself, must of course have drawn up his examination paper with his tongue in his cheek; but his idea, as you have seen, was welcomed with fiendish joy by a number of correspondents. If this sort of thing is to go on, the terrors of the

M

question "Why are you not in khaki?" will be nothing to the terrors of the question "Why don't you go in for Leonard Liebling's examination?" It is little things like this, my dear Joseph, that teach us the noble art of dodging.

Was it Cicero who said he wondered how two professional soothsayers could pass each other in the streets of Rome without winking? Well, you and I, being musical critics, know that two or more of us can never be gathered together without smiling at the gullibility of the public that reads us and takes us for oracles. *We* know how little we know about music; *we* know what hollow humbugs we are. Still, the public must have musical criticism, just as it must have tobacco and alcohol and other piquant poisons; and if fellows like ourselves are not equal to the business, who is? Certainly not the composers. They say the critics know nothing about music. Quite true; but the composers know even less, and as a rule they are shockingly bad judges of the little they know. As I run my eye down Mr Liebling's examination paper, I can imagine myself being able to answer one or two of the historical or critical questions; but I can hardly imagine a composer being able to answer any of them. As a rule, a composer does not worry much about other people's music unless he is either a conductor —in which case he has to know other scores than his own — or a University professor, in which case he has to learn a little in order to be able to teach. Speaking broadly, you will find that the composers who know most about other people's music are those whom the world does not take very seriously as composers. But even the worst of them has a fine sense of superiority to all the others. You remember, no doubt, old Bonaventure des Periers' story of the French gentleman who, excellent Christian as he was, not only loved his neighbour as himself, but loved his neighbour's wife as his own. I know several composers capable of rising to the supreme moral height of loving a fellow-composer's wife as their own, but not one of them capable of loving a fellow-composer's music as his own. That's too much to expect of anyone.

If the composers were to become critics, then, they would make even a poorer show than we ignoramuses do. *We* at least start out without any prejudices. We know nothing about music, and our only concern is to bluff the public into believing that we do. So I advise you, Joseph, to deal as much as you can in generalities. These are pretty safe; it is when you venture into the definite that you are playing with fire. Be particularly careful about musical terms; it is best, indeed, to carry a little pocket dictionary to concerts with you for reference when you get out of your depth. It was by neglect of this elementary precaution that I once very nearly committed a " howler " of the most ululant kind. I spoke of some pianist or other playing Bach's Tomato and Fugue in D minor. Fortunately

for me the head compositor's little girl learns
the piano, and he had seen this very piece lying
about a day or two before; so he altered it to
Toccata. I was furious next day at what I took
to be a misprint; but when I looked it up in the
dictionary I lit a cigar and sent up a silent
smoke-offering to heaven and the head comp.
Of course when the comp. chaffed me about it
I pretended that "Tomato" was a slip of
the pen; but I don't think he believed me.
You may think it odd that I should muddle
up tomato and toccata; but there is a kink
in me that makes me peculiarly prone to
what I may call cibarious errors. Believe
me or believe me not, Joseph, but for years
and years I thought a haggis was a Scotch
musical instrument, of the same family as the
bagpipes.

Fellows like us, Joseph, really ought to club
together and erect a statue to the man who
invented that useful phrase, "a slip of the pen."
It can be made to cover a multitude of journal-
istic sins. Perhaps you have noticed with me,
however, that slips of the pen on the part of
musical critics have not been so plentiful this
last year or so as they used to be. You see,
under the powers vested in the military author-
ities by the Defence of the Realm Act, licensed
premises almost everywhere close at nine-thirty;
and as few concerts end by that hour, a fruitful
source of what may be called induced error
among musical critics is removed. But opportunities for showing our ignorance are still all

too plentiful. We are expected to know everything; and the slightest fall below omniscience is counted unto us as a crime. I have already told you, I think, of the provincial critic who, discussing the Pathetic Symphony without knowing that the composer had been dead a couple of years, said that if Tchaikovski would only attend to this, that, and the other—keep off the drink and be good to his ailing old mother—he might some day write a really good work. That was a classic blunder; but we are all of us liable to fall nearly as low. For the life of me I can never quite remember the difference between Schubert and Schumann,—which of them it was that wrote the *Erl-King* and which *The Two Grenadiers*; and to make matters worse, there is another F. Schubert, who is quite distinct from the fellow of the same name who wrote the *Carnaval*. Then again, I am always puzzled to distinguish between the saxophone, the telephone and the gramophone. *You* may know which of them it is you play with a bow and which with a plectrum, but I'm hanged if I do. I once wanted to make a splash with my knowledge of the physiology of singing; but at the last minute I couldn't remember whether the little red thing at the base of the tongue was the epidermis, the epiglottis, or the epigastrium; so I just wrote "epi" and made a horrible smudge, and left it to the "comps." to get things right—which they did. But there is hardly a difficulty of this or any other kind, Joseph, which bluff will not see you safely through. A musical critic is like Madame Humbert's safe: so long as people are not allowed to see inside it, there is no limit to the riches they will believe it to contain.—Yours always, E. N.

A CRITICISM AND SOME LETTERS

THE SORT OF THING A CRITIC HAS TO GO THROUGH

The Criticism

"LAST night Miss Ethel Winchester gave a piano recital in the Town Hall. If not equally successful in everything she undertook, Miss Winchester at any rate showed that she is a young player of some promise. Like many young people of the present day, she has a technique so remarkable as to make one wonder how she has managed to acquire it in so short a time. It would be unfair to so young a pianist to expect from her an equal ripeness of understanding or feeling; one can only hope that the intelligence she certainly exhibited in one or two of her pieces will develop as she grows older. Some of the music she undertook was evidently more within the scope of her purely pianistic powers than of her spiritual comprehension; it may be doubted, indeed, whether such a work as the great *Hammerklavier* sonata of Beethoven (op. 106) is not beyond the understanding of any performer of Miss Winchester's years. It says much for her courage that she attempted it; it would perhaps have been an even greater tribute to her wisdom had she resisted the temptation. In the works the intellectual message of which lay nearer the surface of the notes, such as the *Spring Song* of Mendelssohn and the *Marche Militaire* of Schubert-Tausig, Miss Winchester did very well indeed. Some Scarlatti and Couperin pieces were given with considerable charm. In the F sharp Impromptu of Chopin, however, she was perilously near coming to grief. Her memory failed her, and though an impartial listener could not help admiring the never-say-die spirit that carried her through to the end without an actual stoppage, he might still be permitted to doubt whether the notes of her own ingenious invention were quite as good as those that Chopin hit upon. Apparently the trouble came from insufficient practice of the work. Miss Winchester should take a leaf from the book of the after-dinner speaker, and carefully prepare her impromptus.

E. N."

I.—The Letters

" Dear Sir,—I wonder how you can have the heart—or shall I say the cheek?—to write about any young and deserving musician the way you have written about Miss Winchester: but I notice that you are always brutal towards young people. If I had a nature like yours I should be sorry for myself. I suppose your liver was worse than usual on Tuesday night. I may add that I do not know the concert-giver personally, and was not at the recital in question, but my sense of justice moves me to send you this protest. 'Fiat Justitia.'"

II.—An Anonymous Postcard

" I suppose the young lady you slated yesterday is not a personal friend of yours. If she had been one of those 'comely contraltos' who 'pressed your hand,' you couldn't have found words to express your admiration for her."

III

"Dear Sir,—Why are you always so hard on pianists? I notice that you never have a good word for any of them. Surely a good pianist is as admirable as a good singer or violinist? In my opinion Miss Winchester bids fair to be one of the finest pianists in England. I am proud to sign myself 'Her Teacher.'"

IV

" Sir,—Is it not time you gave some poor woman a chance? If a male pianist had played as divinely as Miss Winchester did on Tuesday, you would have grovelled at his feet ; but because she is a girl you can do nothing but pour out your horrible masculine venom upon the poor shrinking creature. For me her playing, so thrilling, so truly womanly, was a symbol of the great spiritual work that we women have been called to do in the world—a world at present dominated, but not for much longer, by you soulless brutes of men. Music, the refining art *par excellence,* is *our* art, not yours.

You men look at it through the purblind eyes of the intellect; to us women it is the purest language of the heart. That is why a man is *incapable* of criticising a *true woman's* playing; he is like someone listening to the unfolding of *a great and holy mystery* in a language he does not understand. If Miss Winchester were of *my* mind she would horsewhip you publicly. When we women have the vote we will see to it that women musicians are criticised only by women. Only soul can understand soul.—In utter contempt *for you and all your sex,*

'Tabitha Catt.'"

V

"Dear Sir,—I feel I must write and thank you, in the name of true art, for the sound and well-deserved trouncing you gave to the presumptuous young person who bored us all at the Town Hall the other evening—a trouncing none the less effective, for those who could read between the lines, for the polite sarcasm in which it was conveyed. The only criticism I would venture to make upon *your* criticism was that it was far too lenient. The young lady's vaulting ambition indeed overleapt itself; in my opinion she ought to give up music and take to typewriting or fancy needlework. I did so sympathize with you at having to listen for an hour and a half to such an exhibition of incompetence. I have not the pleasure of knowing you personally, dear sir; but I read with the greatest delight and profit every word that you write, and of course I know you well by sight. I could see from your face that you were boiling with rage and disgust, though of course the ordinary person would not have noticed it. I often wonder how you can be as patient as you are with some of the wretched performers you have to listen to.

"May I add that I am giving a piano recital of my own on the 31st, at which I am playing several of the pieces that were so murdered the other evening? I hope you will honour me with your presence, even if it is only to point out my faults, of which none could be more conscious than myself, though I trust you will find something in my poor efforts to approve of.—With gratitude, Yours sincerely,

ELIZABETH TOOGOOD."

VI

"DEAR MR NEWMAN,—I have just read your notice of my concert, and I feel I must write and thank you before I eat a morsel of breakfast. All night I never got a wink of sleep for thinking what an ass I made of myself at the recital. I made up my mind I would lock the piano in the morning and lose the key. Your article, though I know it to be *too* kind, has quite bucked me up again. It is a relief to me to find you don't think me such a hopeless fool as I thought myself. You were right about the Impromptu. My hat! I never went through such a time as when I felt my memory had side-slipped. What on earth I *did* play after that I don't know. I only hope Chopin wasn't listening to it in whatever place he has gone to. But I felt dreadfully queer all the evening. As soon as I walked on the platform whom should I see but Jack sitting with that putty-faced May Mortimer. What on earth he can see in that insipid, tow-headed thing I don't know ; but anyhow there they were, and I felt she was sneering at me all the time. Then I somehow or other managed to shake a hairpin loose in the Beethoven sonata—I shall remember the very bar to my dying day ! —and it settled in the small of my back, and every time I lifted my shoulder blades for a good whack at the keys it just gave me beans. It all seems quite funny now, but Lord! what I went through at the time! Anyhow I am encouraged to think that you really see *some* good in me after all. I won't chuck the piano key away just yet. I'll work hard and try to do better.

"Yes, thanks ; mother and I will look in on you at tea-time to-morrow, and we'll have some bridge afterwards. Thank heaven there's *something* I can score over you at.—Yours ever gratefully,   Ethel Winchester." [1]

[1] A number of good people seem to have taken all this quite seriously. I received several anonymous letters on the subject, abusing me or sympathizing with me. I permit myself the luxury of quoting verbatim one of the latter sort :—

"Dear Sir,—I have just been a good deal entertained by

your criticism on Miss Winchester's performance, and the indignation it appears to have aroused.

" In the first place I can't understand why it should have given offence, as it seems to me unusually mild.

" It's a pity your correspondence should contain such ridiculous letters, and I don't know which I deplore most, Tabitha Catt's or Miss Winchester's.

" I think the latter about the crudest, slangiest composition it has ever been my lot to read.

" I should imagine her spiritual comprehension must be nil if her letter in any way reveals her character. '*My hat!*' I hope this is not a sample of an educated English girl's letter because, '*Lord!*' if it be, she might as well '*chuck*' away the piano key, as she is hardly likely to inspire her hearers.

" I should like to say how much I enjoy your criticisms altho' I don't understand music.   STARLIGHT."

" Miss Toogood's letter is almost as unspeakable."

HEART AND HEAD IN MUSIC

PEOPLE who believe that in the hour of artistic creation the poet's eye—and presumably also the composer's—is in a fine frenzy rolling, must have been considerably shocked by a recent declaration of Richard Strauss, *à propos* of his *Joseph* : "I work very coolly, without agitation, without emotion even. One has to be thoroughly master of oneself to regulate that changing, moving, flowing chessboard—orchestration. The head that composed *Tristan* must have been as cold as marble." This recalls the old controversy as to whether the actor feels, or ought to feel, his part as if it were real, or should merely "act" it without allowing "sensibility" to obtrude itself—a controversy made famous by Diderot, though he was by no means the beginner of it. Diderot's thesis, as developed in his *Paradoxe sur le Comédien* (written 1770-3, but not published until 1830), was that the good actor does not become the character he is representing to anything like the extent that the ordinary man would imagine. He knows all the time that he is acting ; he never confuses the people around him with the same kind of people in real life, nor does he ever lose the consciousness that the room or the forest in which he is playing his part is not a real room or forest, but merely so many square feet of board with such and such fore-appointed exits and entrances, and so on. Lekain is playing Ninias. After having cut his mother's throat, and while he is giving himself up to the remorse and horror engendered by his act, he sees a diamond that has fallen from an actress's ear. With his foot he pushes it towards the wings for safety—an action implying that Lekain is always conscious that he is Lekain, not Ninias. An actor is killed at the end of the scene, and his body left on the boards as the curtain comes down. In his final struggle with the murderer he perceives that if he dies there and then the curtain will drop plump on his corpse; so he edges his assailant further up the stage, and does not give up the ghost until he has found a spot where he can die without endangering his life. Will you tell me, Diderot would say, that this actor has thoroughly "identified himself with his part?" It is only second- and third-rate actors, he contends, who depend absolutely upon feeling; the first-rate actor creates his illusion in his audience without himself being a victim of the illusion.

Diderot's anti-emotionalist theory, as it has been called, seems to have been in part a revolt against a previous emotionalist theory that had been pushed to absurd extremes. Rémond de Sainte-Albine, for example, lays it down in his treatise on *Le Comédien* (1747) that "Gaiety is absolutely necessary to comedians, whose business it is to make us laugh"; "no one who has not an exalted soul of his own can represent a hero well"; and "only persons born to love ought to have the privilege of playing lovers's parts." Each of the two schools can claim plenty of adherents at the present day; but most people who have given any thought to the subject regard it as settled by Mr William Archer in his brilliant and searching examination of Diderot's thesis, *Masks or Faces? A Study in the Psychology of Acting* (1888). Mr Archer supported some clever *à priori* reasoning by the stories told of the great actors of the past, and by the replies given by leading actors to a comprehensive interrogatory that he addressed to them. And the result, as might have been expected, was to strike a balance between the two extremes; against the anti-emotionalists it can be proved that actors *do* feel the emotions of the characters they represent to the extent of being moved not only to tears, but even to blushes and to pallor; while the anti-emotionalists have the comfort of knowing that whatever emotion the player feels must be held in mastery by him, and played upon as if it were an instrument. The French actor Lambert *père* has summed it all up in a phrase about the necessity of keeping the heart warm and the head cool. It is not an absolutely exhaustive summary, but as a piece of shorthand it may serve.

It is some such process as this, presumably, that Strauss had in mind when he talked of "working coolly," and of Wagner's head being "as cold as marble" when he was writing *Tristan*. But there is a touch of exaggeration in his way of expressing it, as indeed there is in Lambert's.

It is impossible to separate head and heart in this matter. Coolness there must undoubtedly be; but it is a relative coolness—something coming far short of the temperature of marble. Calculation it certainly is not, but rather an unconscious and swiftly-acting sense of proportion, and therefore as much a function of the artistic imagination as is the conception of the emotion itself. Several actors and actresses told Mr Archer that they were much more strongly affected by the tragedy of a dramatic character in their private studies than on the stage, or at all events that unbidden tears would flow and unbidden sobs would rise more copiously in the study. This means that the mere sense of being on the stage and having to convey an emotion to the audience in all its fullness yet without inartistic over-fullness caused the actor to exercise a certain restraint upon himself. Tears and sobs that would cause him to lose command of his voice and deprive him of full control over his muscles in general would spoil his performance as a work of art. These excessive manifestations of grief would be natural enough in real life; on the stage they would mar that harmony of effect that differentiates the premeditated and bearable sufferings and catastrophes of art from the unpremeditated and intolerable ones of life. However deeply the actor may feel for the character he is representing, he has always to remember that there are certain things the character could naturally do in real life that *he* must not do on the stage. As Mr Archer

N

puts it, "the mere sight of the footlights tends to beget that 'temperance' on which Hamlet insists" (in his address to the players).

This control of an emotion by the semi-conscious will, and the regulation of the emotion by technique, are the two formulæ for all artistic creation. I have always thought it a pity that neither Diderot nor Mr Archer carried the inquiry beyond the field of acting into that of dramatic singing. The result of such an inquiry would have been to strengthen the case for the "anti-emotionalists"; for the singer has to take even more care than the actor that he does not lose himself too completely in his part; he has to keep always on hand a double stock of what we may call secondary consciousness—that consciousness of Lekain as Lekain, not as Ninias, and of the scene as a stage setting, not a piece of real life, that allowed him to recognize the diamond as belonging to the real actress, not the fictitious character, and to take prompt measures for ensuring its safety. Not only has the singer, like the actor, to guard against his emotion becoming so overpowering as to affect his voice, but he has constantly to watch that he does not let dramatic passion distort his mouth in such a way as to spoil his tone-production; and of course throughout the evening he has to keep a very considerable portion of his consciousness disengaged from the character he is representing, so as to make sure of taking up all his vocal cues at the right moment, striking awkward intervals correctly, and so on.

The thought "I am Tristan," "I am Wotan," must be dogged from first to last by the thought "I am a tenor; I am a bass; I must not only act well, but sing well; I must deploy confidently the notes on which I am sure of my resonance; I must skilfully manipulate the notes of which I am not so sure." Here again, then, we meet with the apparent paradox that the great operatic actor can only convey the feeling of warmth to his audience by possessing in himself an extraordinary degree of coolness.

Nor can anyone doubt that it is so with the composer. Even in the writing of the smallest work there must be a certain amount of detachment on the composer's part from the emotion of it—a certain cool objective selection, rejection, and arrangement of material; while in works on a large scale there must be an enormous amount of this detachment. The artist may be a somnambulist, but he is a calculating somnambulist. The difference between the great artist and the little one is that in the former the calculation itself is inspired, as well as the idea or the emotion. In one of his letters to Frau von Meck, Tchaikovski has an interesting passage on his own method of writing. The germ of the work comes, he says, suddenly and unexpectedly. "If the soil is ready—that is to say, if the disposition for work is there—it takes root with extraordinary force and rapidity, shoots up through the earth, puts forth branches, leaves, and, finally, blossoms." His somnambulistic dream is broken in upon by domestic and other disturbances. " Dreadful, indeed, are such interruptions. Sometimes they break the thread of inspiration for a considerable time, so that I have to seek it again—often in vain. In such cases cool head-work and technical knowledge have to come to my aid. Even in the works of the greatest masters we find such moments, when the organic sequence fails and a skilful join has to be made, so that the parts appear as a completely welded whole. But it cannot be avoided. If that condition of mind and soul which we call inspiration lasted long without intermission, no artist could survive it. The strings would break, and the instrument be shattered into fragments." Once more we find the emotion being coolly and consciously manipulated by the artist. Without this double consciousness there can be no art.

One remark of Tchaikovski's is open to misunderstanding. He admits that sometimes, when the "inspiration" has lost a little of its heaven-guided urgency, the composer atones for the lack of it by making use of "head-work." It may be true, also, that a few of the bald patches in the works of the great masters are due to some process of this kind. But as a rule the mechanically-made passages in the really big men are the result of their having to fill a traditional form in a traditional rather than a personal way. The awkward moment of this order in the sonata and symphony is the commencement of the "working-out" section. Brahms generally becomes mechanical here, as does even Beethoven now and then. This sort of writing may well be styled "head-work" in a disparaging sense. But it must be remembered that no artist who ever lived, no artist whom we could imagine, could keep "inspiration" going continuously from the first bar of a big work to the last. The composition of a *Tristan* is necessarily the work of many months, perhaps years. The composer must often have to lay down his pen in the middle of a piece of emotional development, and take it up again after an interval of several days or weeks. How does he re-establish the connection here: how does he set the emotional engine steaming on again from the very point at which it had stopped, and at the same pace as before? Obviously by a sort of "head-work," though not precisely of the kind that Tchaikovski means. The composer on these occasions must sit down at his desk in comparatively cold blood; but the mere act of setting his brain to work coolly soon generates the needed heat. He has to do, in fact, what the actor has to do—learn the art of "striking twelve at once," transporting himself into the skin of a character in the brief interval between leaving his dressing-room and making his entry on the stage. Some actors have more capacity for this than others. "It is reported of Kean and of Rachel," says Mr Archer, "that they would at one moment be laughing and joking behind the scenes, and at the next moment, on the stage, raving with Lear or writhing with Phèdre."

Other actors have to induce the requisite auto-suggestion by more or less artificial means. "Macready, as Shylock, used to shake a ladder violently before going on for the scene with Tubal, in order to get up to the proper state of white heat"; others have been known to work themselves into the proper fury for an agitated stage scene by insulting and cursing the "hands" in the wings. A third class of actor can apparently never induce the desired state, do what he will. Have we not here the true parallel, which Tchaikovski missed, with the "head-work" or "heart-work" of the composer? The poorest sort of musician can never develop auto-suggestion, and his music remains cold—either cleverly cold or stupidly cold. Others —or perhaps the same composer at different times—can pick up in a moment an emotional thread that has been dropped days before, or can find the thread by dint of a few moments' tentative work at their desk. And it is here that technique—in itself a cold-blooded matter —helps the composer to generate emotional heat, providing of course he has any to generate. Technique makes a clear road along which the impulses of the brain can realize themselves without let or hindrance. Many a good actor suffers agonies from nervousness for hours before the performance begins, but is at his ease in a few minutes after he has stepped on the stage; his technique carries him over the first difficulties, and then auto-suggestion comes into play. In the case of compositions that are put aside and taken up again a hundred times before they are finished, there must be a vast amount of cool "head-work," as Strauss has said.   But, to repeat, "coolness" as applied to the man of genius, be he composer, poet, actor, or singer, is a relative term.   There is more heat in Wagner's marble than in the boiling oil of all the young composers who have enthusiasm without genius.

THE BEST HUNDRED SCORES

I SEE that Sir William Robertson Nicoll has been adding another attempt to the several that have been made to provide humanity-in-search-of-the-short-cut with a list of the hundred or so books that are absolutely necessary to literary salvation. I have sometimes wondered why a publisher does not try something of the same sort in music. The plain man buys comparatively little music, partly because he knows there is so much excellent stuff that he cannot possibly acquire it all, and so he lets it all go with a sigh. Perhaps if some enterprising publisher and an able editor were to bring out a " A Library of the Hundred Best Scores," with just sufficient editorial matter in them to enable the plain man to find his way about in different periods, to understand the technical and other resources of this epoch and that, and to trace the development from one style to another, he would subscribe for the series in bulk. Such a library, covering the whole art from the middle ages to the present day, could, I think, easily be compressed into a hundred volumes, though of course hardly two people would agree as to the best selection.

One thing strikes us as soon as we begin to think the question over, and that is the greater variety of expression that the musicians show as compared with the men of letters. The world has tacitly consented to take nine-tenths of its writers in specimen instead of in bulk. Dante it is content to have in one poem, or even in a selection from that one. A tragedy or two each of Æschylus, Sophocles, Euripides, Racine, Corneille, and Calderon, a comedy or two each of Aristophanes, Plautus, Molière, Congreve, Wycherley and Sheridan, is enough to satisfy the general appetite. Shakespeare, were we taking our hundred best books to a desert island with us for the rest of our lives, we should like to have complete; but which of us, making up his bag before the voyage, would put in the whole works of any one of the other Elizabethan dramatists if he could find the one work he really wanted published separately? Would not *Faustus* or *Tamburlaine* suffice for Marlowe, and for *The Alchemist* or *Volpone* would we not sacrifice all the rest of the huge volume that Ben Jonson fills in Gifford's edition? Who does not feel that he gets the quintessence of Massinger in *A New Way to Pay Old Debts*, and of Ford in *The Broken Heart*? Does *Joseph Andrews* add so much to our knowledge of Fielding that we would be agitated to find there was no room in the bag for anything else of his but *Tom Jones*? Of the vast output of Voltaire and Goethe, who, apart from the purely historical student, wants much more than *Candide* in the one case and *Faust* and a few lyrics in the other? But the case is very different with many of the musicians. Of the Beethoven symphonies, for instance, the last seven are all indispensable.

Tamburlaine is not different from *Edward II.*, *The Way of the World* from *Love for Love*, *Diana of the Crossways* from *The Egoist*, *The Life and Death of Jason* from *The Story of Sigurd the Volsung* in the way that the fourth symphony is different from the third, the fifth from the fourth, and so on, or in the way that *Tristan* is different from the *Meistersingers*. Either of the plays or poems or novels just mentioned would serve equally well for us to reconstruct its author from ; to attempt to reconstruct Beethoven or Wagner from one work would be to mistake any one room in a house for the house itself. I suppose the explanation of this is to be found in that vital difference between music and literature that constitutes the superiority, in one aspect, of the former—the fact that its language is not a fixed one, that it can be unconsciously expanded by the pressure of a new mode of thought, and that the new resources of vocabulary and technique thus won become in their turn a stimulus to new liberties of thought.

The problem, therefore, not of what to select but of what to reject would be a more puzzling one in the case of music than in the case of literature. In the latter, one work would suffice for the one author; in the former, many composers would have to be represented by several works. But it is worth the while of each one of us to try his hand at making a selection of, say, the best hundred scores—the hundred without which no man's musical education can be said to be complete, the hundred that would present the whole history of music in epitome. To attempt this is to clarify one's critical ideas amazingly. Dr Johnson laid it down, in the case of some poor devil or other who was under sentence of death, that it is bound to clear a man's mind to know he is going to be hanged in three weeks. For any of us to be told that we could select a hundred scores, and no more, from our library, to accompany us to the desert island where we were to spend the rest of our life, would mean putting an edge on our critical sense that it had never known before. Were we restricted, for example, to the music of our own country, I doubt whether we could make up a list of a hundred volumes; we would probably try to compromise by claiming only twenty, and offering to take instead of the other eighty a dog, a cat, or a few white mice. I doubt whether France or Italy or Russia could supply a hundred native scores that anyone who was not patriotic-mad could live with contentedly for the rest of his days. But out of the whole garden of European music what a bouquet could be collected! I myself would begin with a volume—a large one —made up of the finest popular songs of the fourteenth to the eighteenth century, including in these the songs of the Troubadours and the Minnesingers that have come down to us. A second volume would give the essence of the polyphonic music of the period that culminated in Palestrina. I should have, next, two of the earliest operas—Monteverde's *Orfeo* and *L'In-*

coronazione di Poppea—that are now fortunately accessible in a French edition. Then a longish skip might be made in Italian opera, the thread being taken up again with Pergolesi's *La serva padrona* or *Livietta e Tracollo*, Cimarosa's *Il matrimonio segreto*, and Paisiello's *Barbière*. Perhaps five other operas, ending with *Falstaff*, would complete the Italian contribution. In the case of Germany, the problem would be what to leave out: there would be so much of Bach and Beethoven and Wagner and Haydn and Mozart to tug various ways at our heartstrings. But it would be interesting to make the experiment, as I have said, in order to put our affections, faced as they would then be with the imperative necessity of making a decision, to the most drastic critical test they have ever had to undergo. I think we should learn something about ourselves in the process, as a man often learns in a dream something of his real self that he had never, in waking life, suspected to be in him. I feel, for example, that at the last moment I should abandon *Figaro* in favour of the *Seraglio* or *Cosi fan tutte*—certainly the *Seraglio*. Of Strauss, perhaps I should take with me only *Till Eulenspiegel* (or *Don Quixote*) and the *Rosenkavalier*. Of Chabrier—what? Perhaps not even the *España*, but only the little song *L'île heureuse*. Of Brahms, perhaps only the various collections of waltzes. But I find I am wandering a little from my first point. I am not now making up a list of a hundred scores that would serve to epitomize the development of music ; in that list, of course, one of the Brahms symphonies would have to figure. The desert island test is a rather different one. There I should feel, I imagine, happier with the Brahms of the *Liebeslieder* waltzes. For " The Library of the Best Hundred Scores," again, I should certainly have *Tristan*, whereas if I were making up for my own use the " Marooned Musician's Miscellany " I should probably, at the last minute put *Tristan* out and slip the *Siegfried Idyll* in.

THE DECLINE OF SOLEMNITY

A WRITER in a London paper the other day discovered that theatrical London was at present mostly given over to light fare. Sixteen theatres "are already dependent chiefly for their success upon their capacity to make people laugh." Of seven new productions that are promised, "six will base their claims to favour mainly upon their humour and their spectacular qualities"; while "the leading line in every music hall is gaiety." It may be that the majority of people fly to light amusement as an anodyne to their war worries; but one seems to remember having seen much the same phenomenon at work before the war. The explanation of it, I imagine, is simply that it is becoming harder every day to interest a well-fed, well-to-do community in anything serious—especially a community like ours, that has acquired the habit of professing to despise not merely poetry but serious thinking of any kind as "bad form" or "tosh," and of keeping the unpleasantness of life at arm's length by means of irony. If the same process has not gone on to the same extent in music, it is only because there is so little good music of the lighter kind. But that the public is less inclined than of old to go through much hard thinking in music is shown by the gradual migration of audiences from the more solid concerts to those of a lighter type—especially those at which smoking is allowed—and by the tendency to forsake symphonic music for opera in every town that has had good opera during the last few years.

I sometimes wonder whether all tragic art will not ultimately disappear—whether it is not merely a symptom of humanity's spiritual ill-health, as a boil or a rash is a symptom of ill-health of the body. Tragic art may be very beautiful, and yet, in the final analysis, no more than the pearl in the oyster—a product of a diseased tissue. Can we doubt that a race of Olympians, knowing none of our morbid sorrows, would never evolve a tragic art? Humanity, of course, will always have, in the mere facts of death and physical pain, its material for tragedy; but the trend of taste during the last ten years has shown that in proportion as mere life becomes more enjoyable, the appetite for solemnity in art and literature decreases. I imagine that for some time after the war the more solemn forms of art will have small hold upon our public. The artists will still cultivate them, because of the need of satisfying a habit that has become second nature; but for the mass of the people the pleasure of listening to the Ninth Symphony will be nothing to the delight of sitting round a cricket pitch and living light in the sun again. Music will perhaps suffer less than the drama, because, as I have said, good light music is so scarce that the man to whom music is a necessity must either have serious music or none at all.

It was with a sure instinct that Donatello made his St Cecilia so grave-looking a maiden; for music has always been the most unsmiling of the arts. The greatest of its works and men have been overwhelmed with a sense of the seriousness of things. It can show no Aristophanes, no Molière, no Beaumarchais, no one who touches Shakespeare on his lighter side. Perhaps for this its technique and vocabulary are not yet sufficiently developed; we have only to compare Mozart's *Figaro* with Beaumarchais' to realize how much later music is than literature to win command over certain modes of expression. Wit—as distinguished from humorous cheerfulness—was almost impossible in the music of the eighteenth century; that it is becoming possible now may be seen from certain passages in *Carmen*—especially in the scene in which Dancairo and Remendado chaff the captive officer—in the *Meistersinger*, in *Der Rosenkavalier*, and in some of the songs of Hugo Wolf. It is not then, that the nature of music ties it down, more than the other arts, to the serious. It has simply been driven, by sheer lack of control over its own material, to take upon itself rather more than its due share of the seriousness that has been common to all the arts. And that seriousness, I cannot help thinking, will diminish from age to age as human life becomes richer, happier, and more secure. A good deal of the gravity of our ancestors must have been the product of dark and damp houses, excessive toil, incessant anxiety, and, not to put too fine a point upon it, bad teeth and bad cooking. For the *malaise* thus set up the outlet was art; men tried to forget their sorrows by turning them into shapes of beauty that they could hug and caress. We may surmise that many an old picture of bleeding and tortured saints was merely the aftermath of an indigestion, and that the gloomy church and school of St Thomas's—one has only to look at an old print of them to feel the damp and the cold creep down one's spine—played a larger part in the shaping of Bach's religious music than he himself knew—perhaps as large a part as religion itself.

It may be said, of course, that tragic art is not necessarily the immediate product of tragic experience. That is quite true. Art is not life, but an entrancing game played with the forms and colours of life. The pre-requisite of all appreciation of art is that the mind shall have no doubt whatever that it *is* art,—that there shall not be too close a correlation between the artistic expression and the reality it transfigures. If this correlation becomes too close, it wounds. We used to laugh at the humble souls in the gallery who hated the stage villain so violently that they not merely hissed him in the theatre but assaulted him when he came out. But I have seen, during the present war, highly cultured people break down under certain music that in ordinary times would have been to them simply impersonal art, but that now dragged them back into the realities of life. I myself have been sickened in the concert-room by a simple song of Rachmaninov's—about a recruit that was taken for war and did not return—that at any other time would have no more been able to overleap the border-line between art and life than *Orfeo* or *Don Giovanni* can.   To argue that because there is misery in the music there must be misery in the composer is like arguing that because there is pepper in the broth there must be pepper in the cook.   The poet's well-known phrase about poetry being emotion recollected in tranquillity is decisive on this point : and there is an interesting passage in one of Tchaikovski's letters—himself one of the most morbid of men—in which he combats the popular notion that the unhappiness of the composer is to be inferred from the gloom of his music. On the contrary, he says, the composer in the act of creation, and by virtue of the act of creation, is in a state of ideal happiness.   But we may accept all this and still feel that the original thesis remains untouched—that it is out of some earlier unhappiness that the tragic mood is born.   We talk about artists in amazing ignorance of them as men ; only occasionally is it that we know enough of them to trace the connection between their bodies, their lives, and their way of thinking.   As a rule, even had we the necessary data, our present psychology would be too clumsy to probe the secrets of the connection.   We are safe enough with an obvious pathological case like that of Leopardi ; but a Wagner, bare as he has laid himself, eludes us. I myself think that the gloom of much of Brahms' music is to be explained, not, as some German critics explain it, by the fact that he was a Holsteiner, a compatriot of Hebbel, but by the facts of his heredity and upbringing—the elderly, ailing mother, the poverty, the dark Hamburg tenement in which the child's body and mind were moulded. But we need not posit a direct bodily pre-disposition to the tragic in every case. There is the mental as well as the material environment to consider : in many cases the former may even be of the greater importance. The intense seriousness that settled upon German music in the seventeenth and eighteenth centuries was the result, in large part, of the Thirty Years' War and the poverty and misery that followed it. Bach came half a century after the war ; but it was the artistic repercussion of this, perhaps, more than any personal experiences, that made of him so persistent and almost morbid a brooder upon problems of sin and death. If the impalpable indirect pressure of the sufferings of a past age could thus predispose men's souls to life-weariness, surely when humanity, living in ease and comfort and health, forgets the spectres that haunted the imagination of its ancestors, it will cease to take as its highest ideal the art that, seen from Olympus, is no more than the crying of frightened children in the dark.

MUSICAL HISTORY IN A.D. 2217

A FRAGMENT

"THE epoch at which we have now arrived in our historical survey—the early years of the twentieth century —is one of the most interesting in the development of music in England. At that period, English music might be said to be neither child nor man, but merely hobbledehoy. It was suffering acutely from growing pains—pains which it did not always understand, and of which, in consequence, it sometimes took a gloomier view than the circumstances warranted. It was also making desperate though partly unconscious efforts to get out of its system certain poisons that were corrupting its blood and stunting its growth. To readers of the present day, these poisons, that have so long ceased to trouble the body musical, will be hardly known even by name. At the proper place in our history we shall describe the causes, the symptoms, and the consequences of some of them, such as the prima donna, the star tenor, the fashionable violinist, and the exploitation of concerts and of performers by the makers of alleged musical instruments. Here we must give a paragraph or two to one of the most virulent of these old-time musical poisons—the triennial festival.

"Research has established that these strange

institutions mostly held their sway in the early autumn. Such records as we have of them are to be found in the public writings and the private letters of a race of beings—now happily extinct—known in their day as musical critics; but between the public and the private opinions of these people on the subject of festivals there is some discrepancy. In public they condemned them as being one of the main reasons for the backwardness of England in music as compared with other nations; but from the correspondence of these critics, and from such records as have come down to us of their conversation, it appears that in secret they rather enjoyed what they frowned upon in public. It seems that on these occasions they met a number of agreeable people —there were apparently some such even among their own class—whom they had not seen for a twelvemonth previously. The Three Choirs Festivals, held in rotation in three small cathedral towns that were demolished in the Japanese invasion of 2064, were especially popular with the critics. The work, though exacting, was not too heavy a burden, and by the more ingenious among them could be rendered less onerous to themselves by sundry devices, of which the secret is now lost. A diligent search in the files of the Patent Office of the nineteenth and early twentieth centuries has failed to bring to light any record of these devices; so it is to be presumed that they were more of the nature of a traditional and secret lore that passed from mouth to mouth among the initiated, rather than precepts committed to writing, public or private, where they might have met the eye of other than members of the craft. These Three Choirs Festivals were more especially liked by the critics because of the many pleasant walks in which the towns in question abounded; as one of the confraternity is said to have expressed it: The festivals would have been very jolly if there hadn't been any music to go to.

"As to this, of course, their posterity cannot speak. But we know enough of these extraordinary institutions to realize both the harm they must have done to the cause of music in England, and the touching simplicity of soul of our forefathers. From the researches of the Chinese musicólogue Whang Fu it appears that the triennial festival of the nineteenth-twentieth century was a sort of toy given by the public to certain prominent citizens to play with. It was never thought necessary that these citizens should know anything of what was going on in the musical world as a whole. They were simply men of business who had deserved well of their fellow-citizens for some reason or other —perhaps by amassing a fortune by providing the community with grateful and comforting beverages, or by a knowledge of the subtleties of the law, or by having inherited land and cattle from their fathers; and for these services the other citizens allowed them, once every three years, to take into their hands the music of the town. As might be expected, these festivals generally exhibited, on the part of those who managed them, a knowledge neither of music nor of musicians. The latter lack was mostly shown by the preposterous fees paid to conductors and performers, many of whom would have had considerable difficulty in earning half the amount elsewhere. The festival managers' ignorance of the world of music made them, needless to say, very chary of going outside the established reputations, either among performers, or, which was more serious, among composers, with the result that most festivals had the air of being at least twenty-five years behind the times. The managers liked to hear again the works they had been accustomed to hear from childhood, and the managers' wives the works they had sung in when they were girls. Certain faded old works appeared again and again in the programme like an obsession. These festivals, too, were apparently times of national mourning: most of the works that were performed dealt at great length and much lugubriousness with such subjects as sin and death and the general misfortune of mankind in being alive on this earth at all. In some places a particular composer would seem to have specialized in manufacturing these depressing concoctions for a particular area. Thus in the records of the Three Choirs Festivals there appears with great regularity the name of one Parry: and a private letter preserves the remark of a musical critic, in the spring of one year, that it was about time Parry was sickening for another oratorio. There is also preserved a remark, not quite clear to-day, to the effect that at any of these festivals *Parry vaut bien une messe*; but it has been pointed out that the composer in question is not known to have written any masses, and also that the remark occurs occasionally in the form of *Paris vaut bien une messe*, Paris being the old name of the city that is now the capital of the western Chinese Empire.

"The festivities seem to have been first suspended and then slain by the European war of 1914-1944. For one thing, the war led to a demand for greater business efficiency : and it was recognized that just as a musician could not be expected to know enough about the making of cordial drinks to run a business of that kind, so a maker of these drinks could not be expected to know enough about music to run a festival. Moreover, the war, by giving people so much real death to think about, had cured them of the habit of dwelling morbidly on the mere artistic idea of death ; and as for sin, it was felt that after so prolonged a period of suffering and self-denial, humanity could be forgiven if it turned its thoughts more exclusively to the enjoyable things of life, and"

. . . . .

(Here, unfortunately, the fragment ends.)

THE GRAMOPHONE IN THE PAST

I WAS mitigating the rigours of a railway journey the other day by a reading of Villiers de l'Isle-Adam's novel *L'Eve Future*, and was amused by the speculations the author puts into the mouth of Edison, who is one of the characters of the book. Some of these speculations are of considerable interest to the musician. Edison has just invented the phonograph (*L'Eve Future* dates, I think, from about 1883), and Villiers imagines the great man to sit wondering why so simple an invention was not made by some of the scientists of the past, and regretting that some of the most famous sounds in history were thus left unrecorded. How interesting it would be, he muses, if we could now hear, in the original tones, the *Fiat lux*, some of the dicta of the Garden of Eden— such as "It is not good for man to be alone," or "Increase and multiply"—one or two of the oracles of Dodona, or the utterances of the sibyls, or the precise sound of Joshua's trumpets before the walls of Jericho, or the cry of the bull of Phalaris, or the sigh of Memnon at the dawn, and so on. Many other famous sounds might, with a little luck, have been recorded. What would we not give now, for instance, to hear on the gramophone the actual noise made by the

Roman Empire when it fell, or the original swan-
song? The tones and sayings, again, of the
mystic world that we should like to hear again
as they sounded at first!—the announcement of
the Good Tidings, the Salutation, the Sermon
on the Mount, the " Hail, Master!" the Kiss of
Judas, the *Ecce homo* of the prefect, and so on.
Then Edison turns his thoughts to photography.
" How nice it would be now if we had a few
good photographs, taken at the moment of the
phenomenon, of Joshua making the sun stand
still, or some ' Views of Paradise taken from the
place of the Flaming Sword,' or the Tree of
Knowledge, or the serpent, etc. ; or a few views
of ' The Deluge, taken from the top of Mount
Ararat'; or of the Seven Plagues of Egypt, or
the Burning Bush, or the Passage of the Red Sea ;
or authentic picture postcards of Prometheus, the
Danaïdes, the Furies, and others." What an
excellent object lesson, Edison thinks, would a
photograph of a torture scene in one of the
prisons of the Inquisition be, especially if it could
be synchronized with a phonograph reproducing
the cries of the sufferer! (This was written
before the days of kinematography, which is
obviously the medium by which we should have
liked all the stirring scenes of history to have
been preserved for us. No doubt when this war
is over we shall have a number of interesting
films "released"; but how many of them could
compare for pure "thrill" with a film of the
Retreat of the Ten Thousand, the holding of
the Pass of Thermopylae, the retreat from

Russia in 1812, or the Battle of the Frogs and Mice?)

More than most people, I think, musicians must regret that the gramophone was not invented, say, about the end of the sixteenth century. It would have been useful even before then : it would have spared us a lot of speculation and a lot of blundering as to whether the Greeks ever employed harmony, and as to the mediæval rendering of plain-song. But from 1600 onwards there are a multitude of points upon which the gramophone could have enlightened us—what the first operas of Caccini, Monteverde, and the rest of them really sounded like, how Bach filled up his figured bass when accompanying his own works at the cembalo or the organ, whether a Strad violin sounded as exceptionally beautiful when it was first played upon as it does now, or whether time has added something to the richness and purity of its tone, what the old-style way of conducting, against which Wagner fought, was really like, and precisely how much flexibility there was in his own handling of the orchestra ; and so on and so on. Above all, we might learn by this means what we shall never know now—whether the great singers and instrumentalists of the past were really as great as their contemporaries thought them. I am sometimes asked how the performances of the Carl Rosa Company in the heyday of its first success under Carl Rosa would compare with the best of our English operatic performances of to-day. No one, of course, can say, because one's standard becomes more exacting with time. The probability is that many of the most admired performances of the past would be thought rather little of by the connoisseur of 1918. I am aware that people who heard Grisi, Mario, Tietjens, and the rest of them swear that no such singing is to be heard to-day. But obviously they heard these singers in their own enthusiastic and relatively inexperienced youth. Would they think as highly of them could they hear them now, after many years of constant refining and subtilizing of their musical ear? The Knights of the Middle Ages—and still more their ladies —thought there never had been and never would be such brawny fellows as they ; yet the average suit of mediæval armour is too small for the average man of the present day. Richard Cœur de Lion, I imagine, could he return to the earth, would think twice before he "took on" Hackenschmidt or Carpentier. Who can be sure that Paganini himself, under similar circumstances, would impress us as much as Kreisler or Ysaye? Paganini used to create an effect by breaking, in view of the audience, all the strings of his violin but one, and then playing a composition solely on that one. Mr Chirgwin does the same thing, except that he walks on with a fiddle possessing only one string from its birth—just to show there is no deception. I wonder how Paganini would come out of it to-day in a contest with Mr Chirgwin, each of them being compelled, for fairness's sake, to play not only his own music but that of the other. Paganini might score a point or two with the variations on the Austrian hymn; but what would he make of *The Blind Boy*? What would be the voting of the gallery of the Hippodrome after the contest?

Can we be quite sure, from the ecstatic descriptions of mere literary men like Heine, that Paganini was as marvellous as he is alleged to be? Burney thought such singers as Farinelli incomparable. But Burney never heard Caruso, or Jean de Reszke, or Chaliapine, or Tamagno. If he could hear these now, what would he think of Farinelli? The gramophone, had Edison been born a couple of centuries ago, might have helped us to answer this and similar questions. The great singers of the eighteenth century may have seemed so great only because their auditors had never heard any greater. For musical effect, it must be remembered, is subjective as well as objective. As much depends on who and what the hearer is as on what the music is: Cetewayo would not have seen the beauty in Debussy's *Pelleas* that M. Jean-Aubry does. The Edison of Villiers' story, indeed, speculates upon this very point. When Joshua's men blew the trumpets, it was the walls of Jericho, not the Jews or the Canaanites, who fell down. The walls evidently perceived something in the tones that human ears did not, and though it may be true that walls have ears, we can hardly suppose these to be as delicate as ours. The probability is that the Jewish trumpet-playing was so excruciatingly bad that only dull material things like the walls found anything impressive in it, just as the coal-heaver in the gallery at the Hippodrome would be bowled over by a piece of bad singing that would leave a musical critic cold. The whole question with regard to the performances of the past is whether their auditors, not having had the multitude and the variety of our experiences of musical sensation, could have had anything like our delicacy of taste. We cannot trust their unsupported evidence; we might be able to trust good gramophone records of the performances.

THE RECORDER OF SILENCES

I WAS at work in my study the other afternoon when a couple of visitors were announced. I was told that one of them wanted to see me on a matter of the utmost scientific and artistic importance; the other gentleman, apparently, was only accompanying the real caller. The latter, accordingly, was shown up to my study alone. He was a little elderly man, with the look of a born visionary; in his hand was a huge roll of papers.

He plunged into his subject at once.

"I was greatly interested, sir," he began, "in a recent article of yours in which you spoke of the benefit it would have been to humanity had the gramophone been invented a few hundred or thousand years ago—an article which, sir, if you will permit me to say so, has found no more admiring readers anywhere than in the very select community of scientists and artists in which I at present reside."

I bowed.

"That article has emboldened me to come to you, sir," he went on, "in the hope that I may interest you in an invention of my own, that, no doubt you will agree with me when I have explained its nature and its working to you, will be the long-desired complement of the gramophone."

I suppose I looked a little puzzled, for an

eager look came into his eye, and a note of tremulous excitement into his voice.

"Let me begin at the beginning, sir," he said. "I have throughout my life been a collector of negatives."

"Aha!" I said to myself. "Now I see the nigger in the wood-shed!" And aloud: "I am very sorry, but I am not even an amateur photographer, so it would be a waste of time on your part to attempt to get me to buy anything in that line."

"You misapprehend me, sir," he replied with dignity. "I use the term negative in its strict sense of the opposite of the positive. I was first fired to adopt the fascinating hobby of collecting negatives by reading in some American writer or another (it may have been Artemus Ward) of a man in the States who was the proud possessor of a hole that came out of a handkerchief that once belonged to Charles Dickens. At first I was a mere imitator, collecting holes and absences and lacunæ and long-felt wants of all descriptions: among my most cherished possessions I may mention the gap made by the Greeks in the walls of Troy, and the rent the envious Casca made. But in time I began to take a line of my own. Why, I said to myself, should an instrument not be invented that should be the complement of the gramophone, recording not sounds, but silences? You, sir, as a musician, will, of course, appreciate the value of the silences in the music."

"I do," I said, feelingly. "I have been to many a concert at which the silences were all too few. I have often longed for a form of musical composition in which, instead of the notes being the rule and the silences the exception, the notes should be the exception and the silences the rule."

"A very desirable thing, I have no doubt," he said; "but that is not quite what I have had in my own mind. I have dabbled in music myself, sir, and I think you will bear me out when I say that, though silence is, strictly speaking, the negation of sound, it may sometimes be not a negative, but a positive, element in composition: that is to say, there are certain silences in certain works that are in every way as eloquent as the notes."

I looked at him with interest, for he was now talking the soundest sense.

"You are quite right," I said. "Many people have perceived the value of short silences in the performance of music. Some artists make use of them quite unconsciously, being guided only by instinct. One of the differences between a bad performance on a piano-player and a performance by, say, Ysaye or Nikisch, is that while the former is rhythmically continuous, and therefore mechanical, the latter is full of infinitesimal silences at the end of salient phrases— silences that intensify the hearer's anticipation of the coming phrase by an insensible delay in the delivery of it. But composers have been comparatively slow to see the value of silences

P

in composition. Everybody knows the effect of the long silences, punctuated only by an occasional note, in the passage that succeeds the introduction to *L'Apprenti Sorcier*. But effective as these are, they represent only an elementary use of silence in music. Beethoven does the thing much better, for he makes his silences part of the vital tissue of his music. His *fermate* are really silences just made audible; and you will remember how Wagner, in his essay on conducting, makes Beethoven say to his conductors: 'Hold thou my *fermate* long and terribly!'"

"Quite so," said my visitor. "There are certain silences, both in music and in the ideal performance, that we remember as positively as we remember the notes. Now you will be pleased to hear that I have invented an instrument for recording these frequent silences, not as they normally occur in the course of the piece, but without the surrounding notes. That is to say, if you want, some evening, to hear, not the notes of the passage in *L'Apprenti Sorcier* to which you have just referred, but the silences alone, with all the significance they could have in the finest performance, my instrument will give them to you. You will be hearing, not mere empty nothing, but a nothing more full of eloquence than sound itself; and just as you now sit at the piano and play, not the whole of a work, but some extra luscious bar or two of it, so you will be able to sponge out from your consciousness all the notes of the work, and savour simply the great moving silences of it."

I began to feel puzzled again, but he gave me no time to speak.

"And I have been able to do," he went on, "what the inventor of the gramophone has not been able to do. I have made my instrument retrospective—or retro-auditive, if you like the term better. It will reproduce most of the significant silences of the past. You gave a list of the historic sounds that Villiers de l'Isle Adam would have liked to have heard. What would he not have given to hear such an historic silence as "But He answered nothing"? I have not dared to attempt to recapture and record that silence; but with others I have been perfectly successful. How does the old poet describe the death of Roland?" he asked.

"When Roland died, a great silence was through all the earth," I quoted.

"Well," he said triumphantly, "I have recorded that silence, and some day you shall hear it, together with the second, third, and fourth speeches of 'Single-Speech Hamilton,' the confessions that no end of murderers haven't made, and—one of the subtlest and most baffling of silences, this!—what the monkey said to the parrot. If you will just cast your eye over this," he said, unrolling his papers and showing a fearsome collection of designs and figures, "you will get an idea of how the instrument is constructed."

Just then the other man who had been wait-

ing downstairs came up, looked at me apologeti-
cally, and laid his hand on the shoulder of the
scientist. "Come on, old boy," he said affec-
tionately, "it's nearly five o'clock and I have
to get you back by six."

BACH IN THE OPERA HOUSE

BACH would no doubt have some curious sensations could he walk into Drury Lane one fine evening and hear his *Phœbus and Pan* as Sir Thomas Beecham gives it. He might not be very much surprised at finding it turned into a sort of opera, for more than one of his secular cantatas may have been given in much the same form before his own eyes. But he would wonder at the general ingeniousness and beauty of the setting, and still more at the audacity with which his French Suites had been raided to furnish forth a ballet. He would have enjoyed as much as we do the rusticity of Mr Herbert Langley's Pan, and would have laughed till his old wig fell off at the Midas of Mr Mullings, a creation of genius that, in its bucolic Hanoverian grossness—suggestive of some jolly grinning bumpkin out of Fielding or Smollett—goes one better than anything of the sort that the Leipzig of the seventeen-thirties could have shown. But what would astonish and depress poor Bach would be the revelation that it was Pan and Midas, not Phœbus and Tmolus, that the audience really liked : in other words, that the whole object of his cantata had miscarried.

The note in the programme tell us, as all the biographies do, that " the cantata is an allegory. Phœbus stands for Bach and the serious school, while Pan typifies the lighter composers, whose music tickles the ear without stimulating the brain"; and that "under the character of Midas, Bach satirizes a certain Scheibe, whom he had rejected for an organist's post in Leipzig, and thus provoked from Scheibe's pen some bitter attacks on the tedious intricacy of his music." But is it not about time we began to re-examine all these *clichés*? That Bach meant to get his knife into Scheibe, in retaliation for a little flesh-probing from that lively young man, is beyond question. But Scheibe was no fool, and so far as I know there is no evidence to show that he was a cad. It has always been the way with composers and their friends to attribute a critic's dislike of the composer's work to merely personal reasons. Bach was as bad-tempered an old boy as the organ-loft has ever produced; and he was as absurdly sensitive as Wagner to the criticism of smaller men than himself. No doubt it would seem incredible to him that Scheibe *could* have any other reason for objecting to his music than the fact that Bach had plucked him in the examination for an organist's post: but nobody who understands the psychology of composers in relation to critics will accept that as evidence. No one to-day can read Scheibe's *Critischer Musikus* without feeling that, whatever he may have been as an organist, he was a very able man; and no one to-day who is not an utterly blind Bach worshipper can deny that there was, and still is, a good deal of force in his criticism of Bach.

The great man, was, in truth, a little given to over-elaboration, not only in his vocal style, as Scheibe said, but in his organ style. Like all artists who come as the climax of a great tradition, he tended at times to be over-flowery : the medium in cases of this kind is so wonderfully plastic that there is always the temptation to manipulate it to excess for the sheer love of realizing one's power over it. Critics of to-day point to Max Reger's excess of decoration as a sign of decadence. They are quite right : and the same phenomenon is visible in the architecture of decadence. But candour compels us to admit that Bach was sometimes perilously near touching decadence himself. Scheibe was not the only critic of his who thought his love of decoration was too often inclined to run riot. What honest musician of to-day, as he plays through the chorales in Bach's church cantatas, does not now and then feel that the harmonization is a trifle over-luxuriant? What student of the organ chorale preludes does not sometimes have the same feeling with regard to the arabesque into which Bach whips the plain line of the hymn melody? It was only the fact that Bach was a greater genius than Reger, with a profounder nature and a more copious fund of ideas, that saved him from paying to the same extent as Reger the penalty of the artist who comes in at the height of a tradition and finds it affords him endless scope for the decoration of a solidly fixed form.

Now Scheibe's criticism was of Bach's vocal style, which he found over-elaborate, sometimes to dullness. Here again, ought not posterity to do Scheibe justice? Instead of historian after historian repeating the parrot cry that Scheibe must have been wrong because he was only a critic, and Bach must have been right because he was the composer of the *Matthew Passion*, the B minor Mass, and a few hundred other masterpieces, would it not be as well for sober reason to recognize that Scheibe had some grounds for his objection? It was not long afterwards that music as a whole turned away in weariness from the intricate ornament of the instrumental school that came to its climax in Bach, and sought relief in the simpler tissues of Haydn and Mozart. I take it that Scheibe sensed, long before then, the change that was bound to come over the spirit of music; and some credit is due to this young man of twenty-three that he should have done so, and that in a town like Leipzig, where conservatism held its most solemn court on its most ponderous throne. And that Scheibe was right and Bach was wrong is proved by the attitude of every audience that listens to *Phœbus and Pan* to-day. It is Phœbus and his lackey, Tmolus, who are now the bores; it is the high-falutin style that Bach deliberately put forward as the quintessence of pure taste in music, as opposed to the popular, merely ear-tickling rusticity of Pan and Midas, that now puts homicidal thoughts in us as the arias drag their slow length along. The music of Pan and

Midas is still the freshest of joys to the public
and the student alike. It is the music that
Bach wrote as a refutation of the criticism that
his grand style was stiff and pedantic that is
now felt by all the theatre to be both stiff and
pedantic. As Scheibe saw, the style is not a
good vocal one; it is too instrumental, and it
goes on dreadfully slow feet; who among us,
as he listens to Phœbus maundering interminably
about Hyacinthus, does not groan the wish, as
no doubt Scheibe did, that this curled and
scented "nut" among the gods would "get on
wiv it"? The whole allegory has miscarried:
the wind of the satire has veered round; it is
Scheibe, not Bach, that time has justified. And,
crowning irony of all, Bach himself seems to
have felt that, in despite of his theories, the artist
in him had unconsciously turned out better
music for his sinners than for his saints, as was
the case with Wagner in *Tannhäuser* and in
Tristan. Poor Pan gets it from the judges for
his aria *To gladness, from sadness, song waketh
the heart ;* but some ten years later, when Bach
wanted a jolly aria for the Peasants' cantata, it
was this song of Pan's that he lifted almost
bodily. In the end he too banked on Pan,
and posterity praises his wisdom.

More than one auditor of *Phœbus and Pan*
must have felt that the proper, the perfect foil
to it, would be *Acis and Galatea,* which, it will
be remembered, was originally given in theatrical
form. Perhaps no two works could be better
chosen to show the differences wrought in the two

geniuses by the circumstances of their lives.
Handel always plays the game greatly, with
the graces he had learned in courts and noble
houses, and with the accommodatingness he
knew to be necessary in one who was appealing
to the larger public. Bach always remained the
great provincial; one sometimes wishes he could
have had some of the *bourgeois* corners knocked
off him by travel. And he was a slave all his
life to the church and its methods in music.
Even when, on rare occasions, he deigned to
relax the moral pressure of his perhaps too
ethical mind, it was for some purely local
function—to laud the new purchaser of an
estate, to congratulate some royal mediocrity,
to sing the praises of Leipzig or of the rivers
of Saxony; and even in the open air of common
life he found it hard to divest himself of his
cantor's clothes. One of the few really bright
things Spitta says in his voluminous *Life* is to
compare the style of some of Bach's secular
cantatas to a dwelling-house made incongruous
by the addition of church steeples to it. Nor
is it in *Phœbus and Pan* that the secular Bach is
seen at his best. In both the *Peasants'* cantata
and the *Coffee* cantata his touch is lighter, his
eye more humorous, his walk less impeded by
his surplice. And both these cantatas, one
imagines, could easily be turned into delightful
stage entertainments. The *Peasants'* cantata
has all the animation of the theatre, well-defined
character types, and proper exits and entrances.
Not only are the songs delicious in themselves,

but most of them are cast in well-known dance rhythms; and they seem to cry out for the accompaniment of the ballet. The *Coffee* cantata has far more humour in its music than *Phœbus and Pan* has at its best; and here again a little of the modern producer's ingenuity could make a quaint little stage piece of it. There are only two characters in it, together with a tenor who plays somewhat the same part as the *compère* in a French revue. I can vaguely see the piece myself in a sort of double setting, with the father and daughter in the foreground, and at the back a crowd of amused spectators, to whom the tenor could address his explanatory remarks. Perhaps Sir Thomas Beecham will think out the problem of this and the *Peasants'* cantata one of these days. Neither of them ought to present insuperable difficulties to the minds that have managed to bring *Phœbus and Pan* into its present delightful shape.

THE WEARY WILLIES OF
MUSIC

LITERATURE, said Heine, is a great morgue, in which one sees laid out the bodies of those one loves. Criticism, we may perhaps say, is a coroner's court, in which inquiry is held as to the cause of death of this or that artist's reputation. But there is an antechamber to criticism, in which amateur coroners dispute volubly, not as to what the subject died of, but as to whether he is actually dead. Some of them even get into the bad habit of holding the inquest before they have caught their corpse. They are particularly prone to this sort of thing whenever there is a new birth: some of them regard it as their bounden duty to offset each event of this kind by making, if need be, a corpse of some respectable person who, in their opinion, ought never to have been born and has already lived too long. "Live and let live" has never been their motto. To this type of mind, all its own feathered fowl being swans, those of other people must necessarily be geese. Your true Brahmsian can no more see any good in Bruckner than a Calvinist can see any good in a Roman Catholic; and as for Hugo Wolf, who impiously dared to dislike Brahms's songs and to write better ones of his own, has not

one of the high-Brahmins of the English cult
explained to us that Wolf must be forgiven
because he was "hard up and disappointed"
at the time? Surely hierarchic toleration could
no further go! Of late years we have had
a similar sort of heresy-hunt with Tchaikovski
as the quarry. The few people in Western
Europe who knew much about Russian music
as a whole knew long ago that it was being
kept out of its inheritance by the extraordinary
vogue of Tchaikovski. Their dislike of
Tchaikovski was therefore simply the inevitable dislike of the villain of the piece by the
sympathizers with the virtuous disinherited
heirs. That dislike necessarily infected other
honest souls as soon as they learned the harm
that had been done the hero: the good fellows
forgot that whatever harm had been done him
was their work, not the supposed villain's.
When Sir Thomas Beecham, a few years
ago, first lifted the veil from the face of
Russian opera and ballet, the dazzling counten-
ances of these ladies made many an honest
critic regard his old love as a frowsy burden
to be got rid of as soon as possible. In
their first enthusiasm, some of these gentlemen
talked as if Wagner's whole existence had been
proved to be an error of Providence now
that Moussorgski and Borodin and Rimsky-
Korsakov had come; and of course poor
Tchaikovski, as the former light of the Russian
harem, had to be promptly bow-stringed and
sacked. One critic, sitting next to me at one

of the Russian ballets, told me he wondered now how he could ever have listened to the Pathetic Symphony. When I asked him to postpone his verdict until he had heard the music of this ballet as often as he had heard the *Pathetic*, he looked at me as if I were a lost soul.

A public like the British, that has no room in its little palace of art for more than one statue at a time, must always be liable to these fits of iconoclasm. When the fit is over it invariably goes outside and picks up what it can still save of the smashed image from the rubbish heap. This, I think, will happen in the case of Tchaikovski. When the novelty of the other Russian music has worn off, a great part of it will be quietly shelved as being, after all, simply average work, while the really great work will appear more and more wonderful, as all really great work does, as time goes on. Simultaneously people will begin to recognize that they have done Tchaikovski an injustice in summing him up under the one invariable formula, and in judging him mainly by the fifth and sixth symphonies, which contain, along with his best, some of his worst work. The critics always fastened their gaze too exclusively on the black in Tchaikovski's garb; a few years ago, when the Pathetic was all the rage, we used to get the most edifying sermons from some of them on the composer's " pessimism." There is pessimism and pessimism, of course; but the mere nervous worry of Tchaikovski hardly deserves the name. Pessimism in art does no man any harm, any more than optimism in art butters his bread or relieves an aching tooth; and certainly no healthy person ever ate a half-ounce the less at supper after the most agonizing performance of the Pathetic. Pessimism is as good a philosophy of life as any other in a world in which nothing is provable and everything depends on who you are and how you look at it; and pessimism is certainly as good a philosophy in art as any other. There has never been a greater pessimist in music than Bach—never anyone who so fondly dwelt upon suffering and death, and deliberately sought out occasions to do so. But you cannot call Tchaikovski a pessimist with any more reason than you can call a crying child a pessimist. He is merely hurt and very sorry for himself. Tchaikovski was simply a man with intervals of neurasthenia, not a man with a philosophy of the cosmos. He cries out as he does not because he is sitting in judgment on the original plan of the universe, but simply because he is afraid to go home in the dark. He is the typical Weary Willie of art—he generally suffers from what the advertisements call "that tired feeling"—and he is a scared Willie in addition. So purely personal and temporary is his neurasthenia, so remote from anything that can be called a philosophy, that when he attempts to philosophize, to make the heroic soul ultimately victorious over Fate, as he

does in the finales of the fourth and fifth
symphonies, he only becomes portentously
tiresome. What gives real artistic value to
his expression of the terrors that gibbered at
him in the night when his nerves were on
edge is that he really saw them very clearly
and has limned them in such a way that each
of us can recognize experiences of his own in
them. For Tchaikovski would not have found
such a hearing for his woes unless humanity
had had similar woes of its own. He was
the first musician to drag out and give voice
to the frightened child there is somewhere in
each of us.

Rachmaninov owes his vogue to a similar
appeal to the weakness in us. In a sense he
is more virile than Tchaikovski : his melodies
fling themselves out with a largeness that shows,
at any rate, they have bone and muscle in
them. But in some ways he is a weaker type
than Tchaikovski, who had moments of delightful humour, exquisite lightness and brightness
of fancy. Rachmaninov's music has never yet
been known to smile. His typical melodies
always go about in black and with the corners
of their mouths turned down—look, for instance,
at the opening themes of the C minor and
the D minor piano concertos, or almost any
of the themes of the second symphony. What
sometimes seems vivacity in him—the finale
of the D minor concerto, for example—is not
really good spirits, but simply the skilled
pianist's exuberance of ornament ; and the

ornaments are only the white lace on the
pall. He has developed somewhat since the
days of the atrocious C sharp minor Prelude
—days when he was a sicker and sorrier and
shallower puppy-with-distemper than Tchaikovski ever was. But though his muscles have
become braced a little since then, he remains
essentially the same—a Weary Willie with
a dash of Werther in him. And the whole
modern race of Weary Willies in music was
begotten by Chopin upon the chlorotic muse
of French and German romanticism.

ON GREEN SICKNESS AND
THE BLUES

A CORRESPONDENT is wroth with me for having referred, some weeks ago, to the "atrocious" C sharp minor Prelude of Rachmaninov. This epithet, I find, has given a good deal of offence. I was severely taken to task for it by a writer in a musical journal, who also told me very plainly what he thought of me for speaking disrespectfully of Chopin, as he thought. So far from depreciating Chopin, I would say that he is one of the four or five great seminal forces in modern music; he is one of the very few composers of whom it can be said that had he not lived the course of music would have been appreciably different. He has been the fountain-head not only of a new melody and harmony, but of a kind of feeling that at its best has given a new subtlety and refinement to our thinking, and at its worst has deluged us, in his successors, with the morbid sentimentalities that are so common in modern music. It sometimes occurs to me that one of the most interesting books that could be written would be a history of bad music—the sort of music that musicians instinctively dislike and laugh at. Such a book might end, for the present, with *The Rosary*; but where would it begin? The book I have in mind would

not deal with merely dull music, but only with
foolish music, feeble music, sentimental music.
A history of this would really be a history of
modern Europe.   The older Europe hardly
knew it: the feebler seventeenth and eighteenth
century composers could write poor music in
abundance, but of a puppy-whine like *The
Rosary* not one of them would have been
capable.   The least of them was too big for
snivelling self-pity of this kind.   For it is the
snivel of self-pity that, in one degree or another,
makes sentimental music what it is: and it is
mainly from the weaker Chopin that this vast
modern flood has come.   Without Chopin we
should not have had, perhaps, Scriabine or
Granados or Debussy or Ravel; or at any rate
these and other men would have been very
different from what they are.   But without
Chopin we should not have had either the
wailing of Tchaikovski in the dark, the whimper-
ing of all the poor little Nevins, or the early-
romantic pose of the "atrocious" C sharp minor
Prelude.

Perhaps I did wrong to call the work itself
atrocious; what is really atrocious is the vogue
of it.   It takes music back to the eighteen-
twenties and thirties, when musicians and poets
and artists all thought it the thing to adopt a
pose that we now derisively call Byronic.   The
C sharp minor Prelude is simply a shallow
young-mannish attempt at profundity.   "What
a vale of tears is this world," it says; "but see
with what dignity I fold my arms, wrap my black

cloak around me, pull my black hat over my brows, contract my brows into a spasm of defiance, and gaze mournfully but still nobly into the abyss that yawns at my feet!" If a hundred poems and pictures and compositions of the Romantic epoch could talk, that is very much what they would say. And what the reader, the spectator, or the auditor feels inclined to say is this: "Nonsense, my little man. You are not nearly as big, not nearly so profound, as you think you are. What you take to be a philosophy of life is only juvenile green-sickness; what you imagine is a reading of the cosmos is only a fit of the blues. A dose of phenacetin or a day's golf, and you will think quite differently. You are not delivering oracles upon life; you are simply retailing the commonest platitudes and deceiving yourself and others by the pomposity with which you phrase them."

It would be a mistake, however, to suppose that these little people—or the bigger people in their smaller moments—fail because they are not greater thinkers. They fail because they are not greater artists. We feel that some composers have bigger brains than others; but it is probable, in the last resort, that it is only the art that is bigger. In point of sheer intelligence and culture, Beethoven could probably not hold a candle to Saint-Saëns or Weingartner; if we feel that he talks more profoundly in his music than they do in theirs, it is simply that he has the gift of endowing the little common stock of human emotions with a beauty of expression that is beyond these others. An artist may even have a false and narrow philosophy of life, and yet, by the very intensity with which he holds it, and the divinity of his gift of uttering it, he may be able to make that philosophy eternally interesting. There can be little doubt that Bach, in spite of his physical burliness and the vigour of so much of his music, had a strain of morbidity in him; and to this morbidity we owe some of the most beautiful of his art. He lived in a stuffy German town, and was bound hand and foot by a religion that, as it was conceived and practised there and then, had also become stuffy: as one reads some of the German religious poetry of that day, or listens to some of its religious music, one longs, for pure health's and sanity's sake, to fling the doors and windows open and let some fresh air in. The dulness of his environment and the long tradition of complaint in German religious music had bitten deeply into the soul of Bach. There has never been any composer so morbidly fascinated as he by the ideas of death and suffering. They hardly need to be thrust upon him; at the slightest hint of them in his text he runs out to meet them, and lavishes on them the whole intensity of his copious nature. But his morbid broodings, if we can call them such, are never sentimental; from that he was saved partly by the power and variety of his artistic endowment, partly by the fact that sentimentality in music had not been born in those days. We may search Bach, Purcell, Mozart, Haydn, and Gluck in vain for a trace of it. Yet it was already in the air in the latter days of the great eighteenth century German music. All this music strikes us as impersonal; in none of it do we feel that the composer is taking us into a corner and begging us to look into his bleeding heart. That sort of thing came in, roughly speaking, with *Werther* in 1774. It had almost exhausted itself in literature before it seized, some half-century later, upon music. There are hints of it in one or two of the slow movements of Beethoven; but it is not until we come to Chopin, Schumann, Berlioz and Liszt that we reach the type of composer whose sensibility is in excess of his capacity to shape it into art, who has a certain amount of nervous irritability left over that makes havoc of the man's life, and there distils a poison that courses back again into the veins of his music, making that, at times, hyper-sensitive, sentimental, self-pitying, gushing. In the line of the big tradition, this current came to an end with Brahms, in many of whose songs we see the last of the great German sentimentalists—for there are degrees of greatness in sentimentality as in everything else. The C sharp minor Prelude of Rachmaninov I take to be the old Byronic attitude struck in modern musical costume. The apparatus of it is very skilfully managed, but it cannot disguise the fact that underneath it all is simply the pose of the pseudo-philosophical frog trying to puff himself out to the size of the ox. Rachmaninov has outgrown this youthful piece of solemn sentimentality. His music, as I said in the article that seems to have caused such heartburning, is almost always unsmiling ; and it is not the mark of a great man to be for ever going about with the corners of his mouth turned down. But the gloom of Rachmaninov's stronger work has often a touch of virility in it that is very likable ; the music never becomes merely peevish and tearful as Tchaikovski's poorer music does. But with the sham heroics, the false-profound of the C sharp minor Prelude, no musician with any sense of humour can have any truck. The enormous temporary vogue of the work is simply a sign that for a little while one touch of green sickness makes the whole world kin.

"PROFESSIONALISM" IN
COMPOSITION

IT is rather curious that while I was writing on our too great readiness to admire everything a classic does, merely because he is a classic, someone in the *Times* Literary Supplement should have been regarding much the same fallacy—more particularly in poetry and painting —from a slightly different point of view. The thesis of the *Times* writer is that at this or that stage in every art, professionalism—by which he means the mere way of saying things that a period or a single master has made easy, irrespective of the value of the things that are being said—is apt to get the upper hand of inspiration. Art implies the more or less traditional manipulation of a medium, for no man can begin writing or painting or making music as if he had never read a book or seen a picture or heard a score; and there always comes a stage at which the medium is manipulated in merely professional fashion, at the expense of the higher faculty of personal invention. Examples of this process are to be found in the greatest artists : the *Times* writer cites, among others, Titian, Tintoretto, Shakespeare, and Beethoven. One result of this professionalism, he goes on to say, is that it spoils not only the artist but the public, that comes to identify difficulty of handling with inspiration, and is inclined to think too little of the art that is simple, direct, and unencumbered with the visible apparatus of manufacture. The public sees the grand manner in many a passage of Shakespeare or Milton that is the merest platitude phrased with professional pomposity; while it looks down on art so artless as that of Blake in his simpler lyrics.

While everything that the *Times* essayist says is true, I venture to think that he is making the error of calling two different things by one name. In some cases the kind of bad art that he deplores really comes from an excess of professionalism; but in others it surely comes from what might almost be called a defect of professionalism. Bad art of the latter type is bad not because professional competence has run to seed, but because the artist is, for the moment, professionally incompetent, as even great artists are bound to be at times. The writer quotes, as an example of professionalism in poetry, the lines in which Wordsworth compares Ellen Irwin to "a Grecian maid adorned with wreaths of myrtle." Wordsworth's own justification of the simile may be put aside: it is obvious that the determining influence in the last line of his quatrain has been the necessity for finding a rhyme to "Upon the braes of Kirtle." The verse as a whole is bad because not only is it manufactured, but it is so unskilfully manufactured that the process of manufacture stares the least instructed in these things in the face. The mere necessity of rhyming often turns the poet into a clumsy mechanician.

Take, as an example, James Thomson's lines (I quote from memory, and subject to correction) in *The City of Dreadful Night—*

> " That not for all Thy power, furled or unfurled,
>   Would I assume the ignominious guilt
>   Of having made such men in such a world."

The last line is plainly the indispensable thing, the backbone of the whole idea. But there are unfortunately not more than three or four rhymes in English to "world"; and the poet, pinned down to the one of these that he has selected as less irrelevant than the rest ("curled" for instance, would not do), has had to manufacture, in cold blood, a preposterous first line to rhyme with his third, written when the blood was warm. Most stanzas in which "world" is an end-rhyme will be found to show traces of a similar process of manufacture. But we can hardly call bad art of this kind professionalism: it is the sheer incompetence that is the very antithesis of professionalism. For the moment, the poet is not even a good enough workman to bluff us, as Shakespeare or Milton, for example, can so often do, into accepting third-rate verse-manufacture as second-rate.

The real professionalism that does all the mischief in art is something quite different from this. At bottom, perhaps, it is nothing more than mannerism, whether personal to the artist or common to a style or a period. Mannerism means nothing more than taking the line of least resistance. In all of us there is a tendency, after much practice of an art, to follow the easy paths in expression that constant work has channelled out in the mind. (Every prose writer has a rhythm that betrays him.) If the substance of a man's thought is strong enough and varied enough to interest us in spite of our frequent detection of the same procedures of style, we speak of his manner. Wagner will serve as an illustration. If the artist's thought is lacking in strength and variety, so that the habits of style fly out at us and irritate us, we speak of his mannerisms, as with Spohr and a good deal of the later Debussy. The dividing line between manner and mannerism is a very fine one, and fortunately we do not require, for our present purpose, to say where or how it should be drawn. It is sufficient to know that there is an unconscious tendency in every artist to find certain ways of doing things that, for him, are the easiest ways; and it is no wonder that when he finds himself in a difficulty, not knowing where he is going or, indeed, where he wants to go, he should stand in the old safe channel for a minute or two and indulge in a pantomime that has at all events the appearance of getting something done.

The supreme example of this in music is Brahms. There have been few composers so full of personal mannerisms; and these were cross-fertilized, as it were, by mannerisms of tradition. He is "the professional" *par excellence*, in the sense in which the *Times* writer uses the word. Music differs from poetry in that a certain amount

of traditional technique has to be learned if a
man is to say easily what he feels it within him
to say; and this traditional technique, where it
is found at its most consummate in a composer
of less than the very first rank, makes him its
slave instead of his being its master.　Brahms's
self-satisfaction in his professionalism sometimes
becomes sheer fatuity.　I am not, of course,
wiping Brahms as a whole off the slate: I am a
sincere admirer of the bulk of his work.　I am
only contending that much of that work that stirs
the professional Brahmsians to ecstasy shows too
obviously the processes of manufacture to be
really good art.　It amounts to no more, as the
Times writer puts it, than saying nothing with a
grand air: or, if I may quote myself, Brahms
frequently goes on talking, talking, talking, until
he can think of something to say.　The pity is
that it is this sort of professionalism that the
conservatoires thrive upon.　The Brahmsians
rhapsodize over the song *An ein Bild* (Op. 63,
No. 3), in which the pianoforte part is made up
out of variations, augmentations, diminutions and
inversions of the first five notes of the vocal
melody.　In theory, no doubt, but in the main
only in theory, this gives unity to the song: an
equal or superior unity could have been attained
by other means, and certainly by a much less
lavish display of the contrapuntal possibilities of
this one fragment.　Moreover, since it is only a
game of skill that Brahms is playing, it can be
played more audaciously than he has chosen to
play it; any intelligent young student, or perhaps

even his professor, could easily introduce this melodic fragment in counterpoint in several other places. The song is not, as the Brahmsians claim, a supreme specimen of the art that conceals art, but a supreme specimen of the art that shows the bare bones of art. It is the mere *braggadocio* of professionalism: skill is used in the first place for skill's sake, and only secondarily for expression's sake. It is only natural that since this is the kind of thing in art that the professors admire, because it is the one thing in art that can be taught, the weaker-minded of the students and of the public should also be hypnotized into admiring it, to the setting up of an essentially false standard of what art really is. The great problem in such an art as music will always be how to give the young composer a technique that shall be adequate to all the needs of his thought, and yet remain the servant of his thought instead of becoming, as it so often did in Brahms, its master. There are a number of books in which the student has set forth for him, in the form of illustrations from the great masters, what the professors regard as the positive principles of composition. It is a pity someone does not write a book on the negative principles of composition, also illustrated from the great masters. What a collection of awful warnings we could make from Brahms alone! In him, more easily than anyone else, we could study the mummifying effects of professionalism on the professional.

BRAHMS AND THE WALTZ

THE old divine who said that doubtless God could have made a better fruit than the strawberry, but doubtless He never did, would have had to find an even richer superlative had he lived to know the waltz. Doubtless man could have invented a more enjoyable little musical form, but doubtless man never did; and unless I am greatly mistaken, it will see a few of the more solemn forms out. Macaulay's New Zealander will have long outgrown such transitory things as the symphony and the opera; but if there is any humanity left in him he will still glow at the first bars of a good waltz. A musical history in those distant days may even have a chapter in which the symphony, the symphonic-poem, and the opera are written about in much the same detached yet wondering tone in which scientists now write of the flora of the pliocene age: we know such things once existed, but we cannot quite imagine what they looked like. The musical historian in the New Zealander's epoch will do doubt point out how in the mental world, no less than in the physical, the larger and more unwieldy organisms have all come to an inexorable end. First went the mastodon and the pterodactyl: then leviathan and behemoth; then the epic; then the three-volume novel; then the English oratorio; then the Dread-

nought; then the Triennial Festival; then—
long after, of course—the opera and the
symphony. The New Zealander may hold that
a composer can say anything that is worth saying in five minutes at the most; and music may
have reverted to the two fountain-heads from
which it sprang—the song and the dance, both
in a highly concentrated form. This stage of
evolution in music will probably coincide with
the abolition of six-course dinners and the concentration of a day's nourishment into a tabloid.

When that time comes, I think the waltz will
still have for humanity a charm that no other
dance possesses. Other dances we tolerate;
the waltz is a necessity of life. It is difficult
to realize that there was a time when the waltz
was not, just as there was a time when tobacco,
so far as Europe was concerned, was not. But
that is simply a testimony to the worth of the
waltz; Nature tried her 'prentice hand on many
charming things—women, wine, tobacco, birds
and flowers—and then she made the waltz.
The composers as well as the public have all
been enamoured of it: I think I am correct
in saying that there is no other dance form
they have so persistently delighted in. They
may turn up a contemptuous nose at other
dances; but most great composers would be
as ashamed to admit they had never composed
a waltz as to have it said of them that they
had never kissed a girl; indeed, a psychologist
might not unreasonably infer that the composers
who have been guilty of the one neglect have

been guilty also of the other—their music generally shows it. In the days when the waltz was just beginning to rear its timid head, Mozart and Beethoven condescended to be aware of its existence. Since then Schubert, Weber, Schumann, Brahms, Chopin, Wagner, Strauss, Tchaikovski, Berlioz, Debussy, Ravel, Glazounov—to name only a few of the men who have made musical history—have all dallied with the waltz at some time or other.

Perhaps they have done wisely, for it may be that the waltzes of some of these men will be remembered when their more ambitious works are forgotten. And we may note a rather curious thing—that it is precisely the giants who have handled this toy with the most delight for themselves and the most charm for us. Nothing, indeed, is more delightful than the giant in the relaxation of his smaller or lighter works—Tchaikovski in the *Casse-Noisette* Suite, Wagner in the *Siegfried Idyll*, Bach in the *Inventions*, Handel in *Acis*, Strauss in one or two of his songs, and—best example, perhaps, of all—Brahms in his waltzes. For Brahms was the most serious of them all; he carried seriousness, indeed, to the verge of dullness now and then; and his waltzes derive a special charm from their mere contrast with his work as a whole—the charm of the occasional smile on a face that as a rule is kept too grim. Sir Robert Peel occasionally smiled, and Daniel O'Connell's description of his smile was "the silver plate on a coffin." The Brahms waltzes are the silver plate on the coffin of the *German Requiem* and the *Vier Ernste Gesänge.*

What is the secret of the charm of the Brahms waltzes—the sixteen for pianoforte (Op. 39), and the first and second sets of the *Liebeslieder?* Partly it is the old story of a big man taking up a venerable tradition and completing it with the aid of all the emotional and technical resources of a later day. It is to the Viennese waltz that Brahms's waltzes are most closely affiliated—not the public-garden Viennese waltz of the Strausses, Lanner and the rest, but the older and more intimate Ländler type that so fascinated Schubert as to make him devote Opp. 9, 18, 33, 50, 67, 77, 91, 127, and 171 of his pianoforte works to it. In the earliest of these, the type may be seen in all its primitive simplicity—the vamping waltz bass, the tonic and dominant harmony, the almost invariable melodic rhythm :

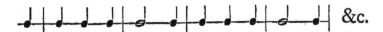 &c.

In the later waltzes Schubert enlarged his rhythmic and harmonic ideas a little, but never to the extent we might have expected. He seems to have been obsessed by the popular origin of the dance, and to have been unwilling or unable to get out of the atmosphere—slightly idealized—of the village barn. All the best of his waltzes seem to cry aloud for further development—for which some of them had to wait for the coming of Liszt. The manifold

R

rhythmical possibilities of the form never dawned upon Schubert: as well as I remember at the moment, there is only one waltz in which he takes advantage of syncopation to obtain what is now one of the most characteristic and delightful variants of the triple rhythm; this is in the thirteenth of the *Valses Sentimentales* (Op. 50):

that Liszt has put to such good uses in the sixth of his *Soirées de Vienne*. But every now and then Schubert hits upon an idea that seems to contain the mood of a thousand modern waltzes in embryo: the opening strain of No. 20 of the *Letzte Walzer* (Op. 127), for instance, is like a sketch for one of the Brahms waltzes.

What Brahms did in the waltz was to give its perfect and final expression to German sentimentality—which term I here use, without any intention of disparagement, to denote a way of feeling that was peculiarly characteristic of the Germany that grew out of the Romantic movement. These people were nothing if not soulful; they could scarcely look at their sweethearts —or indeed at themselves—without tears coming to their eyes. When this mood runs to seed it becomes mawkishness, sloppiness. Brahms does not quite escape this in some of his songs, and others of them are just on the border-line of what is tolerable in the sentimental line and

what is not.   In the first set of the *Liebeslieder*
the balance is beautifully preserved throughout.
Here Brahms has expressed an epoch and a
phase of culture for us with as much truth as
painting or architecture could.   The German
waltz—especially the slow waltz—has always
run largely to thirds and sixths, those great
instruments of the sentimental, that seem to
symbolize the soulful German sweethearts clasp-
ing hands and gazing into each other's eyes.
But though Brahms's thirds and sixths are often
a little sickly in his songs, they are never so
in his waltzes ; no doubt one reason for this
is that the irrepressible blitheness of the rhythm
of even a slow waltz acts as some check on
sentimentality.   The amazing thing is the variety
of expression Brahms gives to seemingly so
rigid a form as that of the waltz.   When the
giants unbend, they do so with a peculiar
graciousness and no loss of strength.   It is
often the brain that is used to roaming at
large over great spaces of thought that works
most happily in the corner of some dainty garden
of art; and each one of the strokes that a
Brahms puts into trifles like the *Liebeslieder*
has a ring about it that would never be given
it by one who had not passed through the
same great experiences.   Had Wagner never
risen to the height of *Tristan* he would never
have developed the tenderness that enabled
him to write the *Siegfried Idyll*; and no
smaller man could ever have written that little
work.   Similarly we may say that had Brahms

never been stretched to the tension of such works as the C minor Symphony and the *Requiem* he could never have relaxed to the charm of the waltzes. It is the superb technique he has won in larger fields that gives him such resource in the *Liebeslieder*; for technique of the highest kind is not merely a means of expressing ideas—it is a liberator and generator of ideas; precisely because the brain functions easily it functions copiously. So we get not merely such quasi-academic things as the double counterpoint of the last of the waltzes of Op. 39, but the more living, more exquisite technique of the *Liebeslieder*, where we can hardly analyse the devices, and certainly cannot account for them, but are simply astounded and delighted at them. Any visitor to this planet who did not know what a waltz is would probably be unaware, at the end of a performance of the *Liebeslieder*, that they are all written in one very restricted form, so multiform are the rhythmical effects Brahms draws from this form. And nowhere—certainly not in any of the songs—has his decorative faculty played about and upon the stem of his themes with such delight as here. How perfectly, for instance, he manages, in the fifth waltz, the falling figure that symbolizes the drooping of the hop-vine, and in the sixth, how exquisite are the suggestions of the bird. For the study of the technique of composition—the perfect adaptation of means to the end—these waltzes are of endless interest. Technically the second

set is as fine as the first, and there are flashes
of inspiration here that are not surpassed by
anything in the earlier waltzes; but imagina-
tively the second *Liebeslieder* are not, on the
whole, on the level of their predecessors. They
share the general fate of "sequels"; either they
merely say as well what has already been said
before—in which case they are superfluous—
or they say it less well—in which case they
are tiresome. In the first set Brahms had
distilled for us the purest essence of German
love-sentimentality; it was hardly worth grind-
ing the flowers again to get this small remainder
of juice out of them. He himself was probably
conscious of this. The choice of the Goethe
lyric for the final song has always seemed to
me a quasi-personal confession that he had
come to the bottom of the cup: to the *Nun,
ihr Musen, genug*, I can imagine him giving
more than one application. At all events, if
he did not do so, we do it for him. For my
part I wish he had not set this poem of Goethe's.
He lengthens the metre into $\frac{9}{4}$, but the effect
is still, in substance, that of the waltz, as, of
course, was his intention; and Goethe's hexa-
meters will not bear this maltreatment of their
essential rhythm. We are face to face once
once more with that failure of the rhythmical
sense in Brahms to which I have referred elsewhere; great as his lyrical technique was, it
was too closely bound up with the folk-song
to be capable of the flexibility that a setting
of the more elastic verse-rhythms demands. We

have only to compare this conclusion of the *Liebeslieder* with Medtner's perfect setting of Goethe's *Einsamkeit* to realize what secrets of poetic rhythm Brahms left unexplored. And the final movement of the *Liebeslieder* is not only rhythmically lame ; it marks the lowest level that Brahms's inspiration has touched throughout the two cycles.

PUTTING THE CLASSICS IN
THEIR PLACE—I

IN *Musical Opinion* for January 1918 "Autolycus" has some frank and sensible things to
say on the subject of the classics : they are
often dull, and it would do some of them no
harm to be touched up a little by a thorough
modern master of orchestration. "Autolycus"
anticipates decapitation for his daring; on the
contrary, we feel inclined not only to leave his
head on his shoulders but to crown it, for "saying
what we all think." I use the term "all," of
course, in its comparative, not its superlative,
sense. There are many solemn gentlemen at
the academies who would not alter a note of
Bach or Beethoven even if it hurt them ; and
the public, of course, accepts reputations in
music as it does in everything else, without
inquiring into the reasonableness of them. But
ordinary sensible musicians must often have felt,
here and there in a classic, that if this little bit
had been written by anyone but Bach or Beethoven they would vote it prodigiously dull,
and that surely Beethoven's brass parts—a
point to which "Autolycus" gives special consideration—need not grate on the ear as they
sometimes do.

We have never had a real iconoclast in music.
We have, it is true, in abundance, young

musicians who dislike Bach or Beethoven or Mozart or Wagner; but their repugnance is so obviously a purely temperamental matter that we take no notice of it. It would really do us good for a genuine iconoclast to arise among us —one who would break graven images impartially and rationally, because he thought graven images bad for our souls, and who would have some sort of workable criterion for knowing a conventional graven image when he saw it, and not confusing it with a piece of individual sculpture. We critics are always complaining of the lack of real originality among composers; but how many critics are really original? The great test of the critic is supposed to be his scent for the right or the wrong thing in new music. I should say that a greater test is his scent for the real or the sham thing in the old music. It is really less difficult to see a modern composer as he really is than to see a classic as he really is; the classic comes to us in such a cloud of transmitted adoration that none of us, do what we will, can turn the same critical searchlight upon him that we do upon Strauss or Debussy. Let us take a couple of specific instances. A few years ago Strauss produced a short orchestral work—a *Festal Prelude* for the opening of a new concert-room in Vienna or somewhere. Virtually the whole of the British press "turned it down," as the vernacular has it: I myself not merely turned it down but stamped on it, for it was a truly wretched piece of hack-work. But there is an early Beethoven

Rondino for wind that Sir Henry Wood is very fond of giving, no doubt for the chances it affords to good wind players to show what is in them. "Autolycus" candidly calls the *Rondino* a dull work. So it is. If one of our young British composers were to produce such a work at Queen's Hall, the critics would with one accord say things about him that would make his ears tingle for a month after. Yet very few of us say, the morning after a concert, that we think the *Rondino* dull; and if we do drop a hint to that effect, it is in a half-apologetic way, as if we knew we were doing the wrong thing in supposing that so great a man as Beethoven could ever be third-rate.

The classics, indeed, get off much too lightly. The young British composer has no chance with even a fairly good work, because it has to stand the comparison in our concert rooms with the very best work of all the great composers of the past and present. But do what we will, the inferior work of the composers of the past sneaks in under cover of their better work. In music there is one law for the rich and another for the poor. Mr Montague Phillips does not stand a ghost of a chance with his *Heroic Overture*, because it is not as good as, let us say, the *Leonora No. 3* or the *Meistersinger* Prelude. But because Beethoven has won the *entrée* to our concert rooms with the *Leonora No. 3* or the *Coriolan*, he abuses his privilege to sneak in with the *Rondino* or the *Choral Fantasia*. Because Mendelssohn has written a very agreeable

Violin Concerto, audiences accept uncomplainingly so disagreeable a work as the *Ruy Blas* overture, a thing so pretentiously commonplace that had Mr Goossens or Mr Ireland produced it last week as his latest work, he would have damned himself in our eyes for at least another five years. Because Brahms wrote finely in the *Alto Rhapsody* and the *German Requiem*, a number of worthy Brahmsians try to persuade themselves that he was equally fine in *Rinaldo* and the *Triumphlied*. The young composer of to-day is not even given the dog's privilege of a first mistake : the classic can get the majority of us to accept almost every one of his mistakes as a Delphian oracle. *Gott in Himmel*, how dull Bach sometimes is ! Yet let anyone show me, if he can, the book in which Bach's occasional faults of dullness and over-statement are frankly laid bare.

I should like to see among us musicians a mind like that of Samuel Butler—a mind that took nothing for granted, accepted no reputation merely on the strength of the noise that had gathered round it in its course down the ages, and that looked at every old work and every old problem with the candid eyes of an intelligent child who saw them for the first time. It would do us good to have some capable person who knew his Bach and Handel inside out and upside down treat them as Ernest Pontifex—who here, of course, is Butler himself—treated the three Greek tragedians ; some one who would apply to the old musicians the questions that Ernest asked in his essay—"Whether the reputation enjoyed by the three chief Greek tragedians, Aeschylus, Sophocles and Euripides, is one that will be permanent, or whether they will one day be held to have been overrated. . . . Their highest flights to me are dull, pompous and artificial productions, which, if they were to appear now for the first time, would, I should think, either fall dead or be severely handled by the critics. I wish to know whether it is I who am in fault in this matter, or whether part of the blame may not rest with the tragedians themselves. How far, I wonder, did the Athenians genuinely like these poets, and how far was the applause which was lavished upon them due to fashion or affectation? How far, in fact, did admiration for the orthodox tragedians take that place among the Athenians which going to church does among ourselves?" And, in connection with another literary epoch, "Which of us in his heart likes any of the Elizabethan dramatists except Shakespeare? Are they in reality anything else than literary Struldbrugs?"

I wish, as I have said, that some devil's advocate would come among us and talk like this about the musical classics. I do not say that we should finally agree with him, but it would do us good, it would clarify our minds and sharpen our critical methods, if we were thus compelled to give good reason for the faith that is in us. I propose to make the attempt in a succeeding article or two.

PUTTING THE CLASSICS IN
THEIR PLACE—II

IT is easy enough, of course, to play the Samuel Butler game with the classics, though perhaps not easy to play it quite so merrily as Butler played it. A philosopher has told us that when you rap your head with a book, and a hollow sound results, it does not necessarily follow that there is nothing in the book. When Butler declared that for forty years he had been "puzzled to know wherein his (Aeschylus's) transcendent merit can be supposed to lie," we take the remark as a light flashed not on Aeschylus's mind but on Butler's. That writer had a wholesale contempt for classics *qua* classics: in words very like those he puts into the mouth of young Pontifex he describes, in one of his essays, "the greater number of classics in all ages and countries" as "literary Struldbrugs" rather than "true ambrosia-fed immortals," —"most classics" being "as great impostors dead as they were when living." But Butler, fascinating as his mind was, had too little imagination ever to be a reliable judge of literature or art. His mind was like his style: it loved to loll about in its shirt-sleeves. It never occurred to him that other men could achieve equal ease and naturalness in a dress suit, and that you can pose as egregiously in your shirt-sleeves as in a uniform—that it is all a matter of constitution and habit. His mind was that of the super-schoolboy—quick, humorous, original, irreverent. But, like the schoolboy, he could never realize when he was out of his depth, and when humorous irrelevance became something like impertinence. Nevertheless, no lover of the Greeks can help being grateful to Butler for at any rate shocking him into trying to give a decent reason for the faith that was in him; and we sorely need some one to let in a similar dry light upon the musical classics. Even the cheeky schoolboy would have his uses for us.

The question, it will be seen, thus becomes one of finding a genuine critical method, equally reliable in its application to the old art and the new. So far from any critic of music in any country ever having attained to such a method, no one has yet realized the necessity of it and begun to try to dig out the first principles of it. We all flounder about with, at best, only half a method, that we apply with the greatest inconsistency to different artists or different styles of art. The fact is that no critic, under present conditions, can do his work in absolute detachment from everything but the pure desire to seek the truth and ensue it. We are not allowed to be mere observers: we are unconsciously driven into being propagandists; and the propagandist, even supposing him to see the truth steadily and to see it whole, cannot be trusted to state the case with absolute impartiality. Do what we will, we cannot resist the primitive impulse to take sides ; the only excuse for us is that we generally persuade ourselves that we are performing a public duty in stripping the last shred of clothing from one composer and refraining from laying even a finger on the superfluous raiment of another. Thus most of us state the case against Handel with all the vigour we can : our excuse is that the public is so unintelligently devoted to him, on the strength merely of one over-rated work, that it is a duty we owe to the truth of art to show them Handel as he really looks to eyes not blinded by tradition. I am afraid we do not state the case against Bach with anything like the same alacrity and thoroughness. Our excuse, if we were pressed for one, would probably be that so long as we are struggling to win for Bach the *entrée* to the favour of a slow-witted public, it would be unwise to lay as much stress on his defects as on his virtues. We gibe at the *Messiah* because we honestly wish people would not make such a preposterous fetish of that work, and because we want to show them how much sawdust there is in the image of their god. But since we want more people to go to hear the *Matthew Passion* and the B minor Mass, we feel that we cannot, all at once, tell them frankly how uninspired are certain numbers in those great works. We should feel like a man giving unnecessarily damaging evidence against his

uncle when the old gentleman was being tried
for his life. We do not perjure ourselves, I
hope, but we maintain a judicious silence; we
may tell the truth and nothing but the truth,
but we do not see any pressing necessity to
tell the whole truth. And so, I am afraid,
it is with most of our criticism. We unconsciously load the dice against a man or a
tendency that seems to us to be making for
something less than the best in art; we unconsciously keep out of sight what might tell to
the disfavour of a man or a tendency that
seems to us to be, on the whole, making for
good.

Our critical method being thus imperfect as
between one composer and another, it is not
to be expected that it should be any more
reliable as between one period or style and
another. We see this most clearly when a
new style, such as that of the modern Frenchmen, begins to disturb the comfortable formulæ
of criticism that we have evolved from the
art of the classics. It takes us some time to
learn the simple lesson, for example, that while
classical music at its greatest, as seen in Bach,
Beethoven, Wagner and Brahms, is in the main
humanistic (or ethical, or philosophical, call it
what we will), there are minds now engaged
in the creation of beauty for whom the humanist
aspect of art has a minor appeal. They are
fascinated by the play of light and colour and
movement upon the surface of things: the
things themselves set up no ethical connotations

in them.   They would say, with Whistler, that
"art should be independent of all clap-trap—
should stand alone, and appeal to the artistic
sense of eye or ear, without confounding this
with emotions entirely foreign to it, as devotion,
pity, love, patriotism and the like."   I do not
propose here to attempt to discriminate between
the truth and the falsity in this way of stating
the problem of art: Mr D. S. MacColl has
done this pretty effectually in his remarks on
the picture that Whistler cites in support of
his thesis — Whistler's own portrait of his
mother.   I desire only to point out that when,
rightly or wrongly, artists begin to see the
world like this, criticism, even if only to confute
them, must at least be able to see as they see.
We can no more apply to Debussy, *en bloc*,
the critical criteria derived from Bach and
Wagner than we can apply to a Japanese print
or a Persian carpet the critical criteria derived
from the Italian religious picture of the
Renaissance.   And lest any thurifer of Debussy
should imagine that this admission justifies all
the extravagances of his admiration of Debussy,
let me hasten to add that the Debussy criteria
are *per contra* inapplicable to the art of Bach
and Wagner.   A critic's personal bias may
be in the direction of the purely decorative
in music ; but that does not destroy, for other
people, the value of the humanistic in other
music.   The genuine critical method would be
comprehensive enough and flexible enough to
deal with them both.

It is inevitable that, our critical criteria being derived mainly from the classics, we should be continually loading the dice against the moderns. In these it is the obvious faults that are the easiest to detect, and so we are apt to lay too much stress upon them. In the classics we tolerantly accept the faults as so much inevitable grit in a dish of generally fine strawberries. Against the moderns we are too much inclined to count only their misses; for the classics we count only their hits. The distinction perhaps does some credit to our chivalry. The classics are old, and we instinctively extend to them the kindly tolerance we always extend to the failings of age. Some day the moderns too will be old, and generous youth will overlook their little faults, and, when they become merely garrulous, wait politely until they have something really vital to say—as we now do during the dull passages in Bach and Beethoven and Wagner. But professional criticism should be an affair not of politeness but of ideal justice. It should not condone a failing in the aged that it chastises in the young. That it so often does so is, I think, simply because its criteria are not sufficiently certain, its perceptions blunted by tradition. The old-style criticism has made many a dint in the armour of the new art. I should like to see some young critic, a partisan of the moderns, retaliate in kind upon the classics. He could show, I think, some analogies between Bach on the one side and Strauss and Reger on the other

s

that would make us good Bachians open our
eyes. The accumulated sentimentality of a
tradition does not run to seed more clearly
in Strauss at his worst than it does in Bach
at his worst. Bach is too often sentimentally
facile as Strauss is, the only difference between
them being that Strauss's overplus of fluent
emotion expends itself on the amorous or the
pathetic while Bach's expends itself on the
religious. The causative factors are the same
in each case—a huge fund of transmitted rather
than personal emotion, that the artist, equipped
with a transmitted technique that is the perfect
correlative of the transmitted emotion, can
manipulate with a quite fatal ease. Bach sometimes runs to an emotional falsity equivalent
to that of Strauss—in those rather unpleasant
dialogues, for instance, between Christ and the
Soul, with their somewhat nauseous mixture
of religiosity and sensuality. And with all our
admiration for the superb work that Bach has
given us in the chorale preludes, what honest
critic can disguise from himself the fact that
here and there the texture of the music shows
the same over-ripeness that we get in the
decadent art of Max Reger — an excess of
harmonic involution and an over-luxuriance
of melodic arabesque? If any young critic
wants a good subject for an article that would
make a stir, I suggest to him "Bach as a
Decadent." He might make fine play with it.

PUTTING THE CLASSICS IN
THEIR PLACE—III

ONCE we realize that, except in their greatest moments, the classics were not super-men, but mere men like those of to-day, the ground is clear for applying to them, in all friendliness and without a suspicion of impertinence, that method of plastic surgery of which I have written elsewhere. Only the sanctimonious prigs among us will deny that occasionally, whether because of a momentary failure of inspiration, a momentary haste or carelessness, or because of the limitations of the technical resources of his time, a classic has set down on paper things that an intelligent modern touch or two would improve. Neither the classics nor the modern composers could logically object to portions of their work being taken in hand in this way, for they themselves have never scrupled to work afresh over each other's music where they thought they could alter it to advantage. We are grateful to them for having done so. Beethoven, meeting Paer after a performance of the latter's opera *Eleanora*, said to him, " I like your opera: I think I will set it to music." That was perhaps not very nice, at the moment, for Paer; but as the result was *Fidelio* and, in the sequel, the *Leonora No. 3* overture, the world has given Beethoven a full indemnity. Bach and Handel occasionally applied plastic surgery to the music of their contemporaries, always improving it when they did so.

Cases like these, it may be said, are cases of the great geniuses improving the work of the talents, and in themselves give no warrant to the talent for trying to improve the work of the genius. The objection is a superficial one. The re-handling of old music with a view to improving it is in a different category from the ordinary "restoration" of a picture or a building. There the restorer cannot do his work without practically destroying so much of the original as he retouches. Music is in a happier case. Whatever retouching a thousand hands may attempt, the original always remains for whoever may prefer it in that form. Let us distinguish, too, between re-arrangement and re-writing. The case for the latter process is sometimes valid enough; but against the former surely nothing can be urged in reason. A composer, even a genius, can sometimes deceive himself strangely as to the best medium in which to present a work. Brahms began his first piano concerto as a sonata for two pianos: the orchestral arrangement was an afterthought. If he could thus deceive himself in the first instance as to the most appropriate colour-setting for his design, is there any reason to regard his second ideas on the subject as necessarily so perfect that no improvement on them can be so much as suggested? Why should we not re-score the orchestral work here

and there, as he re-scored the piano work? In
the clarinet trio (op. 114), he permits, on occasion,
the replacing of the clarinet by the viola. Why
should it not be open to someone else, with a
surer colour-sense than Brahms, to propose yet
another arrangement of it? Dvorak's *Humoreske*
was originally a pianoforte piece. In that form
it attracted no attention for many years. Then
Kreisler made a violin arrangement of it, and the
whole world took it to its heart. The truth is
that the *Humoreske* was essentially, from the
beginning, a violin conception. It was an error
of judgment on Dvorak's part to set it for the
piano, and he should have been as grateful to
Kreisler for correcting his error as a scientist
should be grateful to a colleague for pointing out
a fundamental error of his on a point of fact, or a
fatal flaw in his reasoning. I do not know who
began the practice of playing the E flat Nocturne
as a violin solo; but whoever he was he deserves
the thanks not only of humanity but of Chopin.
Many of Chopin's melodies are obviously so
much more violinistic than pianistic that one
wonders why Chopin himself did not perceive
that fact. He desired the flexibility of rhythm,
the nuance of expression, and the delicacy of
melodic modelling that are the secret of the violin
and of the violin alone among instruments. Sir
Henry Wood is quite justified in arranging some
of the preludes of the "48" for the orchestra:
they have a fulness of emotion that no pianforte
can realize. Who, again, wants to hear Granados'
Spanish Dances on the piano after hearing them

in Sir Henry Wood's orchestral transcription?
I have always felt that, glorious as are the
Goyescas on the piano, we shall never drink the
full rich wine of their beauty until the thousand-
voiced orchestra pours it fourth. I had begun
an orchestral transcription of them of my own;
but I abandoned it when I heard that a friend
whose skill in these matters is far beyond mine
was already engaged upon the work. Who can
doubt that could Moussorgsky hear his *Pictures
from an Exhibition* in Sir Henry Wood's
orchestral arrangement he would confess that
Sir Henry had made him say what he really
wanted to say but could not, on account of the
deficiences of his technique? As Sir Henry
gives it us, the work is more like Moussorgsky
than Moussorgsky himself. Nikisch, I think,
used to alter Beethoven's orchestration here and
there, very much to Beethoven's benefit. Why
should it be supposed that a genius whose gift
was for form and expression rather than colour,
who lived in an epoch when the science of
orchestration was only in its infancy and when
certain instruments had not their present perfection, and who, moreover, was hampered by
his deafness, has hit in every case upon a colour-
combination so ideal that to the end of time it
can never be improved upon?

Nor need the process of re-touching end with
mere re-scoring. Composers cannot greatly complain if now and then someone suggests a slight
alteration in or addition to their music with a
view to improving it, for they themselves have

always been freely critical of their colleagues in this regard. Every time a composer writes a series of variations on another composer's theme, he as good as volunteers to give him a lesson in composition: he implies that his predecessor was blind to the possibilities of his own theme. Paganini would probably not have understood a page of the variations that Brahms has written upon a well-known theme of his, and would have protested against what would no doubt have seemed to him an impertinent desecration. But Brahms was right. He shows us nothing in the theme that was not latent in it all the time, though Paganini had not the wit to see it. Arensky, in his lovely variations on a song of Tchaikovski's in his A minor quartet, only did to the song what Tchaikovski himself ought to have done to it. Mozart has added a great deal to Handel in the *Messiah*; and who will say that he has not, in the main, justified himself? Can any honest musician lay his hand on his heart and say that he does not think that Mozart's accompaniment to *The people that walked in darkness* suggests the atmosphere of the aria more perfectly than Handel's accompaniment does? And that being so, could such a music-lover object to a still subtler realization of the atmosphere by a touch or two of modern orchestration?

No sensible man will object to even more thorough-going manipulations than this of an old composer's music, so long as the manipulations justify themselves in the artistic sense. Grieg added a second part to some of Mozart's piano sonatas, in order, as he said, "to give them a tonal effect appealing to our modern ears." For those who prefer the originals they are still there: but it is the mere pedantry of priggishness to refuse to enjoy the new works that Grieg has made out of them. The question is, were Mozart writing those same sonatas to-day, how would he write them—as he did in the eighteenth century, or more or less as Grieg re-wrote them in the nineteenth? Were Schubert to come to life again and hear Liszt's transcription of his *Hark, hark, the lark*, I do not think he would be offended. I rather think he would say, "Ah, just so! There are some little points in the song that I missed, and that Liszt has rightly seized upon and developed. Especially did I finish off the song in too much of a hurry: Liszt, in all cordiality and politeness, has shown me how I might have made a better ending for it. I am really to grateful him for what he has done." Mozart did not perceive that the Adagio for strings in his second Divertimento would make an admirable prelude to the Countess's song in the second act of *Figaro*. That discovery was reserved for Sir Thomas Beecham. The result justifies him: we now like our *Figaro* better with the Adagio than without it.

I refrain from multiplying instances. I hope I have given enough to show that a modern man of genius cannot do a classic a greater service than by occasionally re-touching the texture of his work where it was originally rather weak or where time has worn it rather thin. The only reservation we have a right to make is that his alteration shall cause the work to fall more gratefully upon our modern ears in its new form than it does in the old.

NONSENSE MUSIC—I

THE girl, said Ruskin, can sing of her lost love, but the miser cannot sing of his lost treasure—meaning, I suppose, that singing implies a certain worthiness as well as warmth of emotion, a worthiness that is present in the girl's grief but not in the miser's. We all used to think that very true; but may not it have been merely because our music and our æsthetic of music were at fault? We had been so long accustomed in this country to regard music only as a branch of religion that it was no wonder both composers and æstheticians failed to imagine even the possibility of a music that was not in some way or other bound up with ethical feeling. Even to-day, music without the smallest ethical implications—such as that of Stravinsky and Bela Bartok—puzzles a number of excellent people like a book in a foreign language that they only half understand; they feel that it must have a meaning for the author and for other people, but as for them, the meaning escapes them. Yet even at the time when this ethical æsthetic was rampant, Wagner was proving that a character could be quite outside the pale of respectable society and yet be capable of singing. As it happened, he actually gave us in his Alberich a miser singing of and for his lost treasure, and a very objectionable gentleman Alberich is. Equally objectionable is Mime, who is also after the treasure and who also manages to sing. Ruskin might have replied that what Alberich and Mime sing is not singing in his sense of the word. The obvious answer to this would have been that in that case it was time he enlarged his sense of the word. We do not expect Alberich to sing exactly like Siegmund: the essential thing is that, whatever it is he sings, Wagner has made him as interesting as Siegmund. The awful heart-hunger of Alberich for the gold, in the second Act of the *Götterdämmerung*, is as sincere and as touching as the heart-hunger of Siegmund for Sieglinde, or of Gerontius for heaven.

What had happened is that music had begun, under Wagner, to extend its boundaries. That extension has been going on ever since, until now he would be a rash man who would say that it is beyond the power of music to express this or that. And music has talked such admirable sense for so long that I wish a composer or two of genius would arise who would make it talk equally admirable nonsense. For really, for so human an art, music has been preternaturally serious : whereas our shelves are covered with masterpieces in the serious genre, the works of genuine and enduring musical humour could probably be counted on the fingers of both hands. There has been plenty of music written to humorous subjects, but it has mostly not been humorous music—not music, that is to say, that we could recognize as humorous apart from its subject. And so far there has been practically no nonsense music, by which I do not mean the mere piling up of absurdity, but that blend of sense and absurdity that we get in Carroll, in Lear, and in Gilbert at his best—the world obviously seen upside down, but still recognizable as the world, and almost as rational seen standing on its head as standing on its feet. Our well-schooled composers will not attempt this sort of thing, partly, no doubt, because routine has smoothed a good deal of original angular humanity out of them, while the composers of the music hall and the lower ranks of musical comedy, however much they may desire to do it, have not the technique for it. For it will require a special technique, as superior to that of, say, *Blest Pair of Sirens* as the technique of *Alice in Wonderland* is superior to that of *The Sorrows of Satan*.

Nonsense music, I am glad to say, has already begun, though it is obviously still struggling with the maladies incident to childhood. As generally happens in art, the first steps along the new path have been taken by composers outside the circle of the elect. Few people in this country, I suppose, know the work, or even the name, of Erik Satie, who was the first composer to specialize in nonsense music. No information about him will be found in any of those dignified publications, the encyclopædias and histories of music. I cannot myself say whether he is still alive or not, though I think he is. He has had the honour of exercising a certain influence upon Ravel, whose father took him in his conservatoire days to Satie, who gave the boy a strange work of his, *Le Fils des Etoiles*, the novel harmonies of which set Ravel thinking. Satie is variously regarded, according to the temperament of the beholder, as a genius, a humorist, or a lunatic. One or two French musicians of standing take him with a certain amount of seriousness. Roland Manuel, who has done a biography of Ravel, has orchestrated Satie's *Prélude de la Porte Heroïque du Ciel*, and no less a person than Debussy himself has orchestrated his *Gymnopédies*. Satie's output is not a large one, and a handful of it taken at random will yield specimens that may be taken as fully representative of the bulk. Some Frenchmen joke with as much difficulty as a Scotsman or a German, and Satie is one of them. Most of us remain, I am afraid, quite blind to the dazzling humour of printing music in red ink and with the bar lines omitted ; our only comment upon a good deal of it is that it would have been still better had the notes also been omitted and then printed in invisible ink. Satie takes some of his laborious joking with the same appalling seriousness as those poets of the Montmartre cafés who are traditionally credited with amusing us with their verses. Those may laugh at *Le Fils des Etoiles* who can ; for my own part I find it merely stupid. There is scope for good fun in this *Wagnérie Kaldéenne*, as its author calls it, but it must be in the music or nowhere, and there is certainly none in *this* music. (I am assuming, by the way, that the music is meant to be funny. I hope I am not making a mistake!) We might raise a laugh at such directions for performance as "*en blanc et immobile,*" "*précieusement,*" "*pâle et hiératique,*" "*courageusement facile et complaisamment solitaire,*" if only there were any humour in the music; but alas, the musical fooling is witless. Elsewhere Satie shows himself a humorist of sorts. His *Sonatine Bureaucratiqùe*, describing a day in the life of an office employé, is quite a pleasant little thing. This is a genre that might be developed—a sort of parody of the more *outré* programme music. It needs to be done with a very light touch, which Satie has at times, but also with an alert musical inventiveness, which he does not always possess; even in so little a thing as this, the amateurishness of the man lets us down badly at times. So with his *Enfantillages Pittoresques*, that are quite charmingly childlike in parts, and in others merely childish.

Satie has, I should say, a good deal of the right sort of topsy-turvy imagination for the nonsense worker, without the musical ability to realize it. Hence it is that his music relies for much of its humour upon its verbal directions. In the *Vieux Sequins et Vieilles Cuirasses* we have what are intended to be burlesque pictures of a Venetian gold merchant of the thirteenth century playing with his treasures, of an ancient Greek dance, and of a child's dream (after some story-telling by his grandfather) of a combat between the Cimbrians and Marius, assisted by

King Dagobert and the Duke of Marlborough. Sometimes there is a really good touch—the grotesquely harmonized bugle call in the Greek dance (*Danse cuirassée*), for instance; but on the whole any smile we can give to the music is as dutifully mechanical as its own humour. He has a vein of genuine burlesque, but it is a small one, liable to give out capriciously at any time. In his *Croquis et Agaceries d'un Gros Bonhomme en Bois* there is a "*Tyrolienne turque*" that gives him opportunities for the sort of comic juxtaposition of opposites in which he delights; but he does not always seize them. In the parodistic *Danse maigre* (*à la manière de ces messieurs*), the musical part of the parody is not so good as the directions for playing—"*sans rougir du doigt*," "*sur du velours jauni*," "*plein de subtilité, si vous m'en croyez*," etc. The *Españaña*, again—a parody of the conventional piece of Spanish "atmosphere"—seems to be always aiming at a humour that it never reaches. When Mr Barry Pain, in *Another Englishwoman's Love-Letters*, took his heroine to Capella Bianca and Festa di Maggio and the Arco di Marmore and Bosco San Giovanni and the Camera d'Orrore, he kept the fun going apart from the mere nonsense topography of words; but Satie's *Puerta Maillot* and *Plaza Clichy* and *à la disposicion de Usted* have nothing in the music to back them up. When, in the *Holothurie* of the *Embryons desséchés* he marks a passage *Comme un rossignol qui aurait mal aux dents*, the joke again remains a merely verbal one. These

Embryons desséchés, however, contain some of his best fooling. They may be described as days in the life of certain inhabitants of the deep. We really seem to get to know the Holothuria ("whom the ignorant call the sea-cucumber") the Edriophthalma ("crustaceans with sessile eyes, that is to say, without stalks and immovable; naturally very sad, these crustaceans live in retirement from the world, in holes dug in the cliffs"), and the Podophthalma ("crustaceans whose eyes are on movable stalks; they are adroit and indefatigable hunters, etc."). We see the Holothuria taking his promenade in the rain, and glueing himself with a sigh of satisfaction to a rock; and we quiver with him when the bit of moss tickles him ("*ne me faîtes pas rire, brin de mousse: vous me chatouillez*"). Best of all is the musical description of the sombre meeting of the Edriophthalma tribe, where a *père de famille* addresses them in mournful tones, and they all weep to the strains of what Satie describes as "*citation de la célèbre mazurka de Schubert*," but that is, of course, a delightful burlesque of the slow section of Chopin's Funeral March. Here there is something for us to go upon. This nonsense has the basis of sense that all good nonsense must have. The trouble with Satie is that as a rule he is not musician enough to stand musical sense on its head, in the Carroll or Lear style, and still keep it recognizable. What he too often gives us is not pure nonsense, but merely damned nonsense.

NONSENSE MUSIC—II

MUSIC is always spoken of as the youngest of the arts. As a matter of fact it has always behaved with preternatural seriousness, as if it had been a few centuries old at its birth. It is only now, when many good people look upon it as being in its decline, that it is really beginning to smile. Perhaps it is becoming young at last; perhaps it is only getting frivolous in its old age: but whatever be the explanation, it is enjoying itself now as it never did before. The classics unbent to a joke very seldom and with difficulty: the moderns are half their time rather ashamed to be caught looking so serious. In part, all this is due to the French revolt, under Debussy and Ravel, against the sentimentalisms and grandiloquences of Romanticism, and against the pathos and bathos of the Germans. Debussy spent a great deal of his time in his later years in larking about in music like a schoolboy: Ravel follows him with his thin ironic smile. In Russia, Prokofiev goes about posing as the *enfant terrible* of music, tweaking the noses, as Mr Montagu-Nathan tells us, of the academics. In France, again, there is Erik Satie, in Hungary Bela Bartok, in England Mr Havergal Brian and Mr Gerald Tyrwhitt, all bent on giving a grimace to music in place of the old set smile on its symmetrically curved lips.

T

The spirit of irreverence is at last abroad in music, thank heaven. We can at last laugh at ludicrous things, and we can even make things not in themselves ludicrous look ludicrous for a moment by giving an absurd twist to them. We are helped in all this first of all by an expansion of harmony and of the harmonic sense that makes a thousand combinations acceptable to us that would have driven our fathers mad, and secondly, by the utter collapse in recent years of pedagogic theory. More true now than ever is it that whatever sounds right *is* right : only the corollary needs to be added that sometimes what sounds wrong is also right in a deliberately nonsensical way. It is mainly by means of absurd or paradoxical harmony that we make our best musical nonsense at present : perhaps melody and rhythm will in time be made equally amenable. Musical nonsense is, of course, as yet only in its infancy. One illimitable field for fun—musical parody and quotation—has so far hardly been touched. The reason is, I suppose, that composers are doubtful as to how far they can rely on the musical memory of their hearers. They certainly have reason to be cautious. I have been at performances of the wordless *L'Enfant Prodigue* at which a number of people have evidently missed the point of the quotation from Mendelssohn's Wedding March. There are no doubt a few who could play through Debussy's *La Boîte à Joujoux* without recognizing the quotation from Gounod's *Faust* ; and I am pretty certain that if one or two analytical programme writers whom

I know were doing a note on Satie's *Embryons
desséchés*, they would be taken in by his grave
assertion that his burlesque quotation from
Chopin's Funeral March was really a textual
citation of "Schubert's celebrated mazurka."
But though musical parody can never appeal
to the multitude, what possibilities of fun there
are in it for musicians! We are approaching
it timidly. Mr Daniel Gregory Mason, the
American composer and critic, has done *Yankee
Doodle* "in the manner of several great composers" (Grieg, Tchaikowski, Brahms, Debussy,
MacDowell [was MacDowell a great composer,
by the way?] Dvorak and Liszt). This is very
good for a beginning. We are reminded of Mr
J. C. Squire's "If Lord Byron had written *The
Passing of Arthur*" and "If Sir Rabindranath
Tagore had written *Little drops of water*,"
though I doubt whether music is yet ripe enough
for burlesques so brilliant as these. But what is
still more needed is the musical parody that plays
the whole game, as it were, off its own bat, as
in Mr Squire's incomparable parodies of Mr
Masefield and others. Of *The Poet in the Back
Street*, or Swinburne writing *The Lay of Horatius*
in his own style, we can almost say that it is
more like Masefield or Swinburne than Masefield
or Swinburne himself. When shall we be able
to point to a parody of Strauss or Debussy and
say that it is more like the composer than the
composer himself? Surely musical parody can
be brought to the same perfection as poetic
parody or pictorial caricature? I do not mean

a mere imitation of the composer's mannerisms
—Wagner's or Elgar's sequences, Debussy's
sevenths and ninths, Grieg's falling thirds, and
so on. That is easy enough. We want this,
but also something beyond it—the capacity to
think as well as talk like some other composer;
the capacity that Mr Squire has for reproducing the very tissue of his victim's thoughts and
feelings.

There is ample scope here for the spirit of
irreverence when that puckish sprite comes to full
consciousness of himself. Meanwhile one or two
gallant attempts are being made to treat life
not merely humorously but derisively in music.
Mr Havergal Brian, in his *Three Illuminations*,
follows in the footsteps of Erik Satie. There
are many facetious touches in the music, but, as
with Satie, we are referred too frequently to the
scenario for the explanation of them. The ideal
music in the absurd genre would be music that
was self-explanatory throughout, once the title
were given us. The perennial charm of, let us
say, *Alice in Wonderland*, is that we have only
to begin by granting the author's premises, and
everything follows from that point as rationally
as in *Madame Bovary*. Really first-rate nonsense
like this is not at all illogical. It has a very
strict logic of its own. John Stuart Mill was
not more consistent in his own way than the
Mad Hatter is in his; it is not in itself any
more credible that a cat should slowly appear
and then grin than that a cat should slowly disappear, beginning with the end of the tail, and

leave only the grin. What is it but a reversal of the engine of logic? My ideal of nonsense music is a music that begins by standing ordinary sense on its head, and then makes it describe accurately and logically the world as seen under these novel conditions. The best beginning possible in this genre has been made by Mr Gerald Tyrwhitt in his *Three Funeral Marches* for piano. I would not say, nor do I think Mr Tyrwhitt would claim, that he has quite realized all at once everything he set out to do; but it is certain that here are three admirable little studies in nonsense music. Mr Tyrwhitt's harmony is like Carroll's story-telling: it is absurd, yet it is logical. Mere harmonic absurdity, in the style that Erik Satie often affects, is so easy that it is not worth doing, if one is going no further with it than that. I cannot smile when, as in the third of his *Sarcasmes*, Prokofiev writes the upper stave in three sharps and the lower in five flats, because what he has written in the two keys is not in itself particularly amusing. This is not being humorous, but only putting on the circus livery of humour. Mr Tyrwhitt, having hit upon a harmonic absurdity, works it out with a sort of Alice-in-Wonderland logic. He gives the face of sense a grimace, but he never lets us forget that there is a real face behind it. In the funeral march for a dead statesman he puts the " Fate" theme from the fifth symphony to admirably ironic uses. The whole thing is curiously expressive of a cynic's smile at the pomposity, the sham eloquence, of the dutiful eulogiums passed upon politicians at the moment of their decease. In the funeral march for a dead canary there is again a most curious blend of seriousness and mockery. The gem of the collection, I think, is the funeral march for the rich aunt who has left the composer her money. It is the first time, I should say, that a funeral march has been marked *allegro giocoso*. There is something inexpressibly comic in the nonsense of the melodies and harmonies: it is as if the happy heir's soul danced for glee within him while he kept a solemn face. And the nonsense, let me repeat, is logical nonsense, the harmonic premises once being granted. We shall hope to hear from Mr Tyrwhitt again.

FUTURIST MUSIC

FUTURIST music, unlike futurist painting, is still so much a thing of the future that, if we except one or two works of Signor Pratella, it has not yet been written, or at any rate has not yet been given to the world. But the ideals of musical futurism have been stated with admirable clearness by certain great men in Italy. As the German military caste aspired to overrun political and social and economic Europe, so these Italian Huns and Goths and Vandals have already their plans docketed for overrunning the whole musical world. The manifestos they have issued from their central bureau in Milan may be regarded as the first army corps of theirs to cross the frontier.

The main body will no doubt follow later with the actual music that is to make an end of virtually every previous composer, from Bach to Bantock, from Schütz to Strauss, from Tubal Cain, indeed, to Tcherepnine. The Attila of this invading horde is one Luigi Russolo, an Italian painter. The more strictly musical head of the army is Signor Balilla Pratella, who has delivered himself at large on the theory of futurist music in a volume (published by Bongiovanni, Bologna), that also contains specimens of his own compositions. But as a theorist, Signor Pratella is sometimes so rational as to

be almost dull. I find the supplementary manifesto of Signor Russolo much more uniformly
interesting. Signor Russolo, as I have said, is
a painter, and therefore peculiarly qualified to
speak on the subject of music. It is safe to
say, indeed, that no mere musician could have
soared to such dizzy heights of speculation. I
had a suspicion, on first reading this manifesto,
that it was a hoax, a very clever *reductio ad
absurdum* of the futurist position; but it is
actually issued from the central bureau of the
futurist movement. It seems that a little while
before this document was drafted there was a
riot at the Costanzi Theatre, Rome, over some
music of Signor Pratella's; and the heirs of the
future had to defend their idol with fists and
sticks and other crude weapons of the past.
In the very midst of the conflict, says Signor
Russolo, "his intuitive spirit conceived a new
art"—which only the genius of Signor Pratella
can create—"the Art of Noise, the logical
consequence of your marvellous innovations."

The music of the past, according to Signor
Russolo, has been hardly better than silence.
With the hand of the skilled theorist he traces
the development of our harmonic sense from
the one or two consonant intervals admitted
by the Greeks, through the timid harmonies of
medieval Europe and the still more timid use
of dissonance in later times, to the bold, free
use of unprepared dissonances to-day. The time
is now ripe for a still bolder flight towards the
seventh heaven of pure noise, which, as Signor

Russolo truly says, is the peculiar glory of the twentieth century, the development of our machines having endowed civilization with a whole battery of noises that were unknown to our benighted ancestors. The ear of a music lover of the eighteenth century would have revolted against many of the dissonances that we listen to to-day with perfect enjoyment. But there is still a vast field of noise to be exploited. As for our orchestras, what are they? Mere combinations of some four or five restricted categories of timbres . . . strings, bowed and plucked, wood, brass, and percussion. "At all costs we must break through this narrow circle of pure sound, and master the infinite variety of noise-sounds." We have heard the harmonies of the great masters too often; they have no message for us but one of boredom. "This is why we take infinitely more pleasure in combining ideally the noises of tramways, motor-cars, carriages and bawling mobs than in listening yet another time to the *Eroica* or the *Pastoral*." A modern concert room is merely "a hospital full of anæmic sounds." Signor Russolo finds it hard, in these places, to maintain his normal niceness of manners. "Pah, let's get out quickly, for I can scarcely restrain my mad desire to make some *real music* here by distributing right and left some good sonorous cuffs on the ear, and by upsetting violins and pianos, double basses and groaning organs. Let's get out." The Italian insurance companies are no doubt doing splendid business among orchestral players since Signor Russolo began to take an active interest in music.

Some *passéists*, as the futurists call the rest of us, will no doubt object that noise is displeasing to the ear. With these impenetrable fossils Signor Russolo has not the patience to argue. Think, he says, of the surprising variety of noises—the thunder, the wind, cascades, rivers, the rustling of leaves, the trot of horses, a carriage bumping on the road, "the solemn white respiration of a town at night, all the noises made by cats and other domestic animals, the gurgling of gas and water in pipes, the borborygms and the rattle of motors, the palpitations of valves, the come-and-go of pistons, the strident cries of steam saws, the sonorous joltings of trams on the rails, the cracking of whips, the flapping of flags." And, of course, the newest and perhaps best noises of all, those of modern war, should not be forgotten.

"Although," Signor Russolo goes on to say, "the characteristic of noise is to recall us brutally to life, the art of noise ought not to be limited to a simple imitative reproduction. The art of noise derives its main emotional power from the special acoustic pleasure that the inspiration of the artist will obtain by the combination of noises." The futurist orchestra is to be grouped into six categories of noise —it would unfortunately take too much space to quote these and their sub-divisions here. As Signor Russolo truly says, "the variety of noises is infinite. We possess to-day more than a thousand different machines, each with its distinctive noise. With the incessant multiplication of new machines we shall some day be able to distinguish ten, twenty, or thirty thousand different noises." And he ends with a passionate appeal to Signor Pratella to give the world some specimens of this new music, and to young musicians to cultivate it on their own account.

It may puzzle the *passéist* reader to imagine what this new sort of music will be like. Signor Russolo himself, not being a musician, of course cannot show us; but I gather that it will resemble the description of the battle of Adrianople that Signor Marinetti sent to Signor Russolo in a letter from the Bulgarian trenches. I regret that I can transcribe here no more than a line or two of this masterpiece: "Choumi Maritza o Karvavena cries of officers clashing together copper dishes *pam* here *pac* over there Boum-pam-pam-pam-pam here there further off all around very high attention Good God on the head smashing chaak! flames flames flames flames flames flames flames Choukra Pasha telephones his orders to 27 forts in Turkish in German Hello Ibrahim! Rudolf hello! hello! actors rôles echoes smoke-decorations forests applause grass-mud-dung-odour I no longer feel my frozen feet odour of mould corruption gongs flutes bells pipes everywhere above birds warbling beatitude shade verdure cip-cip-zzip-zzip flocks pastures dong-dang-dong-ding-bèèè."

That does not seem, at first sight, particularly hard to do; but perhaps there is more in it than meets the eye. We shall look forward with interest to hearing some futurist music before long. All that Signor Marinetti and Signor Russolo have to do now is to give us some hints as to a futurist musical criticism to correspond with this new art. We shall have to make our concert notices tally with the music —in a manner of speaking, make the punishment fit the crime. We may yet live to read something of this kind in our daily papers: "Concert Signor Pratella futurist music help help help police miau miau discord noise holy Moses cries of wounded ambulances lint trepanning cut it out boom bang crash he-he-he-he help help want my money back shut up you fool police Lord Mayor soldiers Riot Act boom slash bang another blood-vessel burst bang bang boom my hat where's your Wagner now? thank God that's over wow wow let's go and have a drink."

FUTURIST STAGING

NEXT year,[1] it seems, is to witness the production at Glastonbury of the choral drama *The Birth of Arthur*, of which Mr R. R. Buckley has written the poem and Mr Rutland Boughton the music. I take it that this is only another name for *Uther and Ygraine*, the text of which, together with a manifesto by Mr Buckley and Mr Boughton on the music drama of the future, was published some two or three years ago. I remember hearing Mr Boughton play the music once, and being greatly taken with it. Of the value of Mr Buckley's drama I am not so sure. It is intended to be a " national " drama—that is to say, because we happen to live in a country that was inhabited, many hundreds of years ago, by certain thick-headed and insanitary people known as the Ancient Britons, we are all supposed to be possessed by a consuming love for them and their ways and their history, and to be thrilled to the bone by the very names of them. For my own part I have never been able to feel that thrill. I suppose it is a fundamental defect in my make-up, but really Merlin and Arthur and the rest of them have never meant as much to me as Agamemnon, or Oedipus, or Hannibal, or Ali Baba, or Paris and Helen, or Potiphar's wife, or a hundred other historical or legendary

[1] 1914.

figures. So I politely but firmly decline to be agitated by anything that happened or didn't happen to Ygraine. The people in Mr Buckley's drama apparently think that it is of the utmost importance to Britain, for all time, that Ygraine should have a baby. To me, and, I suspect, to others, it does not matter two pins whether Ygraine has one baby or five, no babies or ten thousand, or who is the father of any or all of them. Deaths are much more interesting dramatic material than births; since the *Valkyrie* and *Siegfried*, indeed, what we may call the obstetric opera has been rather at a discount.

Every man to his taste, however. I would not willingly do anything to shake the faith of Mr Buckley and Mr Boughton in their offspring. Rather is it my desire to wish them all good luck with it, and especially to commend them for the originality of the proposed staging of the opera. Some particulars of this staging were given by Mr Boughton to a contemporary the other day. The scenery is to be represented by human beings. " For ' Tintagel Castle,' for example," says Mr Boughton, "men of the company will be massed together, dressed in tight-fitting costumes of brown probably. And then women arrayed in green and blue will play the waves breaking on the sea-shore. Everything will be very simple. For instance, the rising of ' Tintagel Castle ' will be suggested by men players all slowly raising their arms above their heads."

I call this sort of staging futurist because we

certainly have not seen anything of the kind
hitherto. Like all good things, however, it has
its roots in the past—though in pointing this
out in the interests of historical accuracy I
would not be understood to imply any lack of
originality on Mr Boughton's part. The glory
of the full application of the principle of human
scenery will not be denied to Mr Boughton,
even though the principle itself is not wholly
new. I understand that the waves that excite
our hilarity in the pantomime or strike terror
into us in melodrama have always been produced by the agency of human actors, who
heave their backs and subside again beneath a
piece of canvas. There is, in fact, a classic
story of a horrible catastrophe at some theatre
one night, the waves being agitated in a manner
too violent and too erratic to be explicable by
any known seismological law. It was discovered that the manager had unwisely introduced a differential tariff among the boys who
represented the sea ; a quarrel had broken out
on the bed of the ocean, and the shilling waves
were giving the eighteenpenny waves a licking.

There is logically nothing to be urged against
this method of what may be called symbolical or
allusive staging. Mr Boughton's method,
indeed, has the merit of superior honesty. He
plays his cards in full sight of the audience.
There was something underground, or at all
events under-sea, in the old-style pantomime
way of representing waves by human beings.
A fraud was being perpetrated upon an innocent

and trusting public. The management said, in effect, "These are real waves," whereas they were not real waves at all. With Mr Boughton everything is above board. He says, "I don't pretend for a moment that these supers of mine are real waves. I only ask you to assume, with me, that they are; therefore the heaving and the billowing may as well be done in full view of the audience. There is no deception." And who will dare to say that this faith in the imaginative powers of his audience will be misplaced? Is not art already full of what the vulgar would call fakes, but what the instructed ones know to be an amiable co-operation between a beguiling artist and a believing public? What is all painting, for example, but a tacit agreement between the painter and us that objects that exist in three dimensions shall be accepted when represented in two, and that moving objects, like the sea, shall be supposed to be in motion even when the canvas is obviously still? Nay, the Japanese go even further than this. Hokusai does not attempt to represent waves as realistically as a European painter will. He just draws a wavy line or two and says, in effect, "Since all painting is only supposing, let us suppose that these lines convey to you, by suggestion, the idea of a river in motion." And if a mere streak of two or three colours can thus be made to represent a lot of waves, why should that privilege be denied to human beings? Surely a man is of more account than a paint brush?

To my thinking, insufficient use has hitherto been made of this power of suggestion in objects. Why should we be always told the whole story in art: why should not something be left to our imagination, our faculty for drawing conclusions? Why should we not be asked to infer the dog occasionally from the tail, the cat from the grin? I have a dim recollection of a system of teaching geography in my youth that may have been only a joke, but I sincerely hope to have been a reality. The children first of all looked at a curtain. This was drawn aside, showing a wooden horse. That was Delos. The curtain fell, and was once more withdrawn, revealing the same horse again. That was Samos. If we had only had our imagination properly developed in childhood by some such method as this, we should be in a better position now to appreciate the originality and effectiveness of Mr Boughton's new system of staging opera.

Everything transitory, as Goethe said, is but a symbol. Why then insist on tedious and futile realism, when a symbol is not only more effective but considerably cheaper? I can foresee many advantages in this new method of Mr Boughton's. Let us suppose that a manager has gone to great expense to get a beautifully painted scene representing a castle. If anything happened to this—if it were lost in transit from one town to another, for instance—the consequences might be serious. It is within the bounds of possibility that that particular opera could not be given that night. But if the castle were re-

U

presented by a number of men putting on the stoniest look they could, the loss or temporary absence of one or two of them would make no difference at all; the audience would at once gather from the gaps in their ranks that it was intended to suggest that the castle was in a state of ruinous disrepair. Everyone knows, again, what trouble there always is in the third act of *Tannhäuser* with the Star of Eve; the stage hand who is entrusted with the management of this astronomical curiosity never *can* get the candle, or whatever it is, to take up its position at once behind the hole in the canvas and stay there. Why not bring symbolism into play here? The Star of Eve is surely the same thing as the Evening Star. All the stage manager has to do, then, is to paste a placard of that respectable newspaper on the spot in the heavens where the Star of Eve is supposed to rise with such law-defying suddenness on *Tannhäuser* nights. And if men can represent waves, why cannot they be trusted to represent horses? It has always been a grievance, of late years, that Brynhilde does not ride her horse Grane into the flames in the final scene of the *Götterdämmerung.* If the horse is willing, Brynhilde is usually not, or *vice versâ;* and between the pair of them the spectator is cheated of something he has a right to expect after paying his money. It is only equine stupidity that makes the horse terrified at the flames and the noise of the orchestra. Why should not the part of Grane be taken at

Covent Garden next year by those admirable
animal impersonators the Brothers Griffiths,
who would, of course, be strangers to stage
fright? Few people, again, realize in a stage
performance the importance Wagner attaches to
the Tarnhelm—the magic headdress that con-
ferred on the wearer of it the power of changing
his form or making himself invisible. Would
it not be much more effective if the part of the
Tarnhelm were played by the Mad Hatter? And
Mr Boughton's human waves—why not have these
parts taken by actors with aqueous names:
First Wave, Mr Rivers; *Second Wave*, Mr
Waters; *Third Wave*, Miss Lake; *Fourth
Wave*, Miss Brook; and so on? Or have
Tintagel Castle represented by Mr Towers,
Mr Wall, Mr Stone, Mr Mason, and Mr
Castle? I am sure the idea contains the
promise of great things.

THE MUSIC OF DEATH

I SUPPOSE we have all been asked some time or other, or have asked ourselves, what is the music we would take with us if we were condemned to live on a desert island for the rest of our lives, and were allowed the choice of only one or two works. It is a question much easier to ask than to answer, because there is an unlimited quantity of music that is very delightful to live with, and to give any of it up would be hard. But the question as to which music we would most willingly die with is perhaps easier to answer, because the possible ground to be covered is much smaller. The question I am proposing, it will be observed, is rather as to the music we should like to hear in our last moments than as to the music we should wish to have played over our graves, or hear played in mourning for someone else. As to this latter the choice is singularly small, as everyone must have felt who has taken part in a funeral or memorial service for the great dead. It is really very hard for a composer to strike the right balance, in a work of this kind, between gloom and elevation. Gloom there must be; but one instinctively feels that the last word should be something that transcends the bitterness of death. The ordinary practice is the reverse of this procedure—to begin and end in darkness, as it were, with a middle section of a brighter kind, in which the spirit that still seeks for grounds for hope may take wings to itself. This is the method adopted, for example, in the Funeral March of Chopin. That method certainly results in a rounded artistic whole; but for purposes of public ceremonial it is not ideal, since it fails to send us away with that gleam of consolation, the half-hope that life may after all be greater than death, that alone can make the thought of death tolerable. Mr Sidgwick, in his delightful book *The Promenade Ticket*, has aptly satirised this formula of composition: "Most funeral marches seem to cheer up in the middle and become gloomy again. I suppose the idea is (1) the poor old boy's dead; (2) well, after all, he's probably gone to heaven; (3) still, anyhow, the poor old boy's dead." I am afraid that I, for one, will never be able to listen again to Chopin's Funeral March without being reminded of Mr Sidgwick's summary. In any case the salon sentimentality of the middle section of that work makes it less appropriate than it might have been to great occasions of public mourning.

There are hardly more than one or two pieces of music, inspired by a purely funerary feeling, that reach the topmost height of art, and of these few, not all are wholly suitable for the commemoration of our great dead. The Funeral March in the *Eroica* loses much of its point when detached from the Symphony as a whole. Wagner's *Trauermarsch* is superb, but for one thing it is too heroic in scale for such dwarfs as ordinary humanity. For another thing, it is essentially a lament over physical beauty vanished and youthful promise broken, and so unmeet for the graves of men whose impress upon the world has been through their thought. Thirdly, it has running through all its noble grief a touch of passionate revolt against the evil that brutalizes the world, senselessly destroying young life at its fairest; and it is not in this mood that we should leave the graveside of our philosophers and poets. There is a beautiful and impressive Funeral March in Mackenzie's *Dream of Jubal*, which ought to be performed more frequently than it is. The words make it peculiarly appropriate for the burial of a soldier. Grieg's elegy upon his dead friend Nordraak begins grandly enough, but, as usual with Grieg, does not develop convincingly. After all there is nothing so fitted for ceremonial mourning as the Dead March in *Saul*. Here tragedy is broadened into a spiritual solemnity; the grief is never merely physically tearful or protesting; and at the end a great consoling hand is laid upon us unobtrusively. It is the kind of music the pitying, wise-eyed gods might have written for mankind.

Of the music not ostensibly funerary in purpose, but obviously inspired by a sense of the mortality of things, there is again not much that one could bear to hear in one's last hour. This is no disparagement of it as art, of course. Tragic art is for the living; the pain of the message must always bring with it its own anodyne in the beauty of the utterance. But one needs to be in the full flush of life to bear the overwhelming flood of tragedy that the artist sometimes pours over us. *Gerontius*, for instance, is for the healthily living, not the dying. Nor could we bear, when the end comes, many another piece of music that is an artistic joy to us now, but that then would have too much of the cold horror of the grave about it. No one at that hour, I imagine, could bear to listen to the frenzied wailing and sobbing of Tchaikovski's Pathetic Symphony. That music does not come from a deep enough well of philosophy; it is too much like the cry of a frightened child being pushed into a dark room. Music so full of the chill terror of death, heard in one's last moments, would almost make the dead drum with their fingers on the coffin lid for release. Nor is the great Death March of the Brahms *Requiem* any more meet for dying souls. Those grisly, uncompromising strains are too suggestive of the horrors of physical dissolution; as one listens to them one can almost feel the damp clay already sealing up one's lips. In all music there is no more terrible suggestion of annihilation than Wolf's song *Alles endet, was entstehet*; but to bear to hear that on one's death-bed one would need nerves of steel. The struggle of the soul with death in Strauss's *Tod und Verklärung*, again, is too realistically terrible; while the apotheosis, grand as it is in the concert-room, is hardly the music one would wish to die to or waken again to. It is too spectacular, too brilliantly lit, too full of the pageantry of a crowd; whereas this is a journey one must make very quietly, and alone. There is a more touching human quality in Ravel's *Pavane for a dead Infanta*, in which a curious pathos struggles through the deliberate restraint of the slowly-moving music, as if hearts were breaking beneath the heavy brocade of those ceremonial Spanish robes.

We shall all have different preferences in a matter of this kind; but had I a choice I think the music I should like to have prepare me for death would be the first movement and the Adagio of Mozart's G minor Quintet. The battle is over and the fight lost, says that divine music; but it was a fight that humanity could never have hoped to win—and how sweet one's tears were, and how exquisite the bliss of sinking back into that fount of being from which we came! The lovely melodies and harmonies of the first part of the slow movement of Grieg's Pianoforte Concerto, again, would, one thinks, soothe any one's dying hour. And for the actual passing away what could be more subtly luxuriant than Chopin's C minor Prelude? Were I allowed to choose the time and the manner of my going, like the old Roman I should open a vein in a hot bath, while an orchestra of muted strings repeated time after time the dying fall of the Prelude, in decrescendo after decrescendo imperceptibly fading away into silence. One can almost savour in advance the voluptuous joy of such a death. And then, on the other side of the Styx, to be greeted by the heart-easing, care-free strains of Mozart's *Eine kleine Nachtmusik!*

ON FUNERARY AND OTHER
MUSIC

WITH the exception of Elgar, none of our composers, so far as I know, has produced any music, inspired by the War, that expresses anything of what the nation feels in these dark days. The *Carillon*, with its fine-strung pride, has been a consolation and a stimulus to the best there is in us. Only out of an old and a proud civilization could such music as this come in the midst of war. It is a miracle that it should have come at all, for Europe is too shaken just now to sing. Never before have we realized the full depth of the meaning of the poet's remark as to poetry being emotion remembered in tranquillity. We may have known that before, but only æsthetically : to-day the saying has a new moral force for us. It is because the time for remembering in tranquillity is not yet that our poets and musicians, as a whole, have failed us ; for the best that is in the best of them we shall have to wait till the raw immediate edge has gone off these horrors, and memory and thought can play upon them in detachment, contemplate them without a pang, and order them into plastic shapes that shall console and soothe. At present, Elgar alone seems able to detach himself from the too painful reality of the moment, and sing of the war and its blood sacrifices as if they were just ordinary emotional material for the musician— which is not to say, of course, that he feels them any less poignantly than the rest of us, but simply that the artist in him gives him the power, denied to the rest of us, of quintessentializing his emotions, of extracting from the crude human stuff of them the basic, durable substance that is art. His two new choral works *To Women* and *For the Fallen*, seem to me well worthy of the title that is to embrace the whole cycle when the third setting is ready: *The Spirit of England*. *For the Fallen*, in particular, is as noble a threnody as modern music can show. As in the *Carillon*, the music expresses at once consolation, courage, and chastening. It is worthy of the sacred dead who have died for England.

None of the wars of the past seem to have produced any really great music. The war of 1870 gave us only Wagner's *Kaisermarsch*—a good enough piece of work in its way, but the merest by-product of Wagner's genius—and the rather empty *Triumphlied* of Brahms. Whatever may be the result of the present War, there will not, I imagine, be songs of triumph written in any of the countries of Europe. We have probably seen the last of the blustering, boastful side of war; even now it survives nowhere, indeed, but among the weaker intellects of the music halls. But if there will be no exultations in music after the War, there will need be solemnities—gatherings in great temples, where men in great numbers can renew for a moment their fellowship with each other and with the dead. Something of our bitterness of spirit, our sense of loss, of defeat by the blinder forces of life, will then have to be poured out in music. What music will that be ? It is strange that out of all the music of the centuries there are still only some two or three works that strike the true funerary note with any power or dignity. Of death music, sorrowful music, the music of lament or of elegy, there is no lack ; but this is not funerary music, and the people have instinctively recognized that fact in their choice of music for public ceremonials for the dead. The difference between the two orders is well shown in a volume of organ pieces entitled *Funeral Music*, that has just been published by Messrs Novello. I myself should not call the final movement of the Pathetic Symphony funeral music. It is too personal an outpouring of grief for that. The essence of true funeral music is that it speaks for us all; it cancels our merely personal emotions, as the occasion itself does ; it reduces all the participators in it to the common human denominator—and a denominator that holds good for the humanity not merely of a country and a day but of all space and all time. The finale of the Pathetic is moreover too terrible in its pain for occasions of ceremonial mourning. We could not bear to take leave of the dead believing that death is so cruel as this. How definite is the dividing line between death music, however great in itself, and true funerary music, may be seen again in the " Trauermarsch " from *Siegfried.* Here too the emotion is too personal ; in our requiems for the great dead it is not the mere individual we mourn for, but the mortality of mankind itself.

It is less surprising that there should be so very few genuine funeral marches when we consider that in the funeral march the composer, even supposing him to have the right idea, has to work with the minimum of material. All the greatest music is common, in the best sense ; it may reveal more of its secret to one soul than to another, but to the humblest soul it has some-thing to say in a language it can understand. But nowhere surely has music to be so common as in the funeral march. As the occasion is too solemn for artifice, and as the music must appeal to what I have called the common human denominator in a great gathering, any wilful decorativeness of melody, any over-sophistication of harmony or rhythm, any too obvious bravado of technique, would be felt at once as bad taste. It would be like coloured plumes on a funeral coach. The composer has, then, to work with the barest minimum of musical means. All funeral marches have much the same melodic, harmonic and rhythmic characteristics, because composers have instinctively recognized this duty of showing us grief in its simplest and yet most universal expression. And when we see how much of his ordinary apparatus the com-poser has thus to surrender, we can understand how severely the task tries him, and why no more than some two or three pieces of funerary music have stood the test of time. Intuitively the common man rejects the funeral march that is too dramatic, too personal, or too petulant in its moan, or that is too small in spirit for a multitude. We have all the external trappings of woe in the quasi-funeral march in the *Lieder ohne Worte* (No. 27) ; but Mendelssohn is here, as generally elsewhere, too small-chested to sing for all humanity. The feminine endings to his melodies seem a worse weakness than usual here; and the march has that air of gossipy familiarity with great emotions—it is as if the composer were *tutoyant* death—that is so irritating a feature of Mendelssohn's religious music. Tchaikovski's funeral march for the piano (Op. 40, No. 3) fails, again, because it is too much like Tchaikovski to be like all humanity, as the true funeral march must needs be. Beethoven's two funeral marches (that in the Piano Sonata, Op. 26, and that in the *Eroica* Symphony), great music as they are in their proper places, are again too personal, too flecked with anger or revolt or pitifulness, to be appropriate for the ceremonial of massed humanity. Anger, revolt, pitifulness—the individual may give way to moods like these as he thinks of his dead, but not a community. Of what moods, then, must the true funeral march breathe? Of sorrow, certainly, but not of sorrow too poignant, too personal, or too local ; for it is not so much the dead we are mourning as death and the inevitableness of death. The dead we celebrate are only a symbol of an endless, age-long procession. And it is because, unknown to ourselves, a great ceremonial mourning raises in us this idea of the vastness of time that funeral marches take on them their slow, inexorable rhythms, their steady uniformity of tread. Melodic, harmonic, and rhythmic reiteration is the mark of all funeral music—unhurrying, repetitive time, for time is the one possession left to the dead. It is largely because the Dead March in *Saul* and Chopin's Funeral March are so rich in what we may call the spaciousness of time that they remain the two unapproachable examples of their kind. In Handel it is a tranquil spaciousness; we feel the world both of the dead and of the living to be very wide, and the cosmic purpose very assured. Handel's march will probably always remain the grandest, the most appropriate for vast gatherings of humanity. It is common in the true sense; it voices the emotions of the humblest hind, yet around its simple lines can crystallize the subtlest feeling of the most complex among us. Chopin's March is only less great because it is more gloomy, but great it undoubtedly is. Chopin gives us once for all the darkness of the underworld. (I am speaking now, of course, of the first and last movements.) What Beethoven was feeling after in the harmonies of the funeral march in the Piano Sonata Chopin achieves in a flash. The middle section of the March is a little sentimental, but not so much so as to be hopelessly out of the picture of the main matter; and, after all, it is of this that we think when we

speak of Chopin's Funeral March. In spite of
its perhaps excessive gloom, it has, like Handel's
March, the great quality of suggesting spaciousness and eternity. These two Marches remain
the finest of all expressions of the funerary spirit
because of the majesty and patience they breathe
—for the dead are very majestic, and very
patient.

THE MUSIC OF FELICITY

ONE would be inclined to say, on *a priori* grounds, that of all the media of human utterance music was the one best fitted for the expression of moods of felicity, for in the notion of felicity there is involved something super-earthly, and of all the arts, music—"sounding air," as Busoni calls it—is the one least clogged with earthly matter. Yet, singularly enough, music is anything but rich in the expression of these moods. That may seem at first sight an exaggeration ; but we shall see that it is not so if we define felicity carefully. It is best defined first of all, as most abstractions are, by exclusion of what it is not. To begin with, it is not mere happiness or good spirits. In the latter, music is inexhaustibly rich ; Bach and Beethoven are full of good spirits of one sort—a rather muscular sort, as befits those great-thewed Titans—while Domenico Scarlatti's music has an exuberance of joy that can find an outlet only in a kind of kittenish gambolling. Music has lost many things in its pilgrimage through the ages, and this particular mentality has probably gone from it for ever. For sheer happiness of another kind there is no music to compare with that of Haydn ; here is the very song of the clean blood's delight in itself ; and here again the music is what it is because it belongs to an epoch before music had begun to grow old and anxious

x

and excessively thoughtful.   It would be almost
impossible, indeed, to find a great composer
whose music does not at times exhale happiness
of some kind.   The composer least rich in this
quality is Brahms.   *"Er kann nicht jubeln"*—
"he cannot rejoice"—was Hugo Wolf's most
biting indictment of his rival.   It is not wholly
true, of course, for the note of exultation is strong
enough at times—in such a song, for example, as
Meine Liebe ist grün; but in the main the
indictment fastens surely enough on the weak
point in Brahms's equipment.   For Brahms is
very like Hebbel in the grayness of his vision of
life.   A gifted German critic, Walter Niemann,
attributes this Hebbel-like quality in Brahms to
the fact that both were Holsteiners—a race that
has been made dour in the course of ages by its
environment ; but in the case both of Hebbel and
of Brahms the determining factors were more
likely early poverty, poor nourishment, and a
childhood generally lacking in ordinary opportunities for laughter.   There are happy men and
women to be found even in Hamburg—the
melancholy, rainy, gloomy Hamburg, as Herr
Niemann calls it—in spite of the Holstein blood,
the Holstein sea, and the Holstein sky.

Everyone, perhaps, would define felicity in his
own way, but to me it seems to imply a happiness
more or less completely detached from the
physical.   Yet this in itself is insufficient to
define it.   No music is so non-terrestrial as the
best of Mozart ; there we have the free play of
beautiful units and lines of sound, a sort of ideal

cosmic harmony that excludes man with all his ugly pains and no less ugly joys. When Mr Wells's Kipps first saw a chart of our internal anatomy, the astonished ejaculation of that simple soul was "Chubes!" Nature is careful to hide from us these hideous mechanisms; she bids us rejoice, if we are wise, in her subtle rhythms and adjustments without enquiring too closely into the rather repellent apparatus that produces them. It is because in music, as Pater said, the form is inseparable from the matter, that music is of all the arts the one that seems to speak the very soul of things, expressing not this idea or that, as Schopenhauer would put it, but The Idea, The Will in Itself. And it is because Mozart's music moves about so light-footedly, with the air of the minimum of dependence upon even such matter as music is bound to admit, that it gives us the sensation of some ideal dance of nature's forces at their most ethereal. In no other music are we so little conscious of "Chubes." Yet though Mozart's music is full of a sort of disembodied happiness, I can recall nothing among it that quite answers to my idea of felicity. It may be that the music is *too* dis-embodied. Felicity implies not merely content-ment, but contentment after striving; and the contentment of Mozart's music is that of a being who has never known strife. The closest analogue to this music in another art is the Hermes of Praxiteles; there too the smile is that of a being that has never known a tear or lived anywhere but in the light.

Still narrowing down our definition of felicity,
we have to exclude from it its next-of-kin—
rapture. Of this, too, music offers us thousands
of marvellous examples. But to examine what
is, I think, the finest specimen of it in all music
—the strains that accompany Brynhilde on her
awakening in the third Act of *Siegfried*—is to
see at once the difference between rapture and
felicity. Rapture implies, I should say, a state
of well-being the very excess of which must find
outlet in action, while the notion of felicity excludes the idea of action. Nowhere in all music
is there anything to equal, for pure joy in the
sense of awakening life, this music of Brynhilde's.
For happiness of its own sort it will probably
be hard to find a parallel to it in any other
art—the happiness of liberated limbs luxuriously
stretching themselves out in glowing sunlight
and mountain air. (Those high and tenuous
violin figures convey an almost blinding sense
of light.) But, as throughout the *Ring*, we feel
everything to be more than life-size; and
through these mighty muscles rapture indeed
may course, but not felicity. One would think
that the mystics among composers would have
poured out in profusion the typical music of
felicity, music in which one felt the delicious
relaxation of all bodily and mental forces, the
glad surrender of the will to a mere delight in
living that seeks nothing beyond itself and the
moment. Yet while the prose and poetical
mystics give us these moods in abundance, the
musical mystics never dwell in them for long

at a time. César Franck often leads us just over the threshold, but stops us when the way into the inner hall of the temple seems clear. The passage in his works which gives me the fullest sense of felicity, of the happy poise of all the faculties of the body and all the forces of the world, is the smoothly-flowing canon that opens the last movement of the violin sonata. German music, curiously enough, is not rich in this kind of thing. Schumann and Brahms attain to it now and then in their songs, but only for a few bars at a time; the most complete example Brahms gives us of it is probably the song *Feldeinsamkeit*; the picture of quiet felicity there would be unbroken but for the dark modulation in the second verse at the words "gestorben bin." In English music the finest expression of this rare frame of mind—perhaps the only expression, and certainly one of the finest in all music—is the short orchestral prelude to the second part of *Gerontius*, descriptive of the beyond-world into which the soul floats in the moments immediately following death. Here we have in perfection the sense of motion without limbs, of the suspension of all thought, all volition, of a passionless ecstacy in the bosom of the sustaining ether. The finest expression of felicity of a more mundane kind to be found in music is, I think, the exquisite E major passage in the love duet of Tio Lukas and his wife in Hugo Wolf's opera *The Corregidor*; I cannot remember any other love music, with the exception of a few bars in the love scene in Berlioz's *Romeo and Juliet*, that so perfectly conveys the sense of the complete absorption of two happy souls in each other, and their complete detachment from all the world. The passage that comes nearest to it is perhaps that commencing "Du wunderliche Tove," in Schönberg's *Gurrelieder*. But to my thinking the purest expression of felicity in all music is Euridice's aria and the chorus of the blest spirits in the Elysian Fields ("E quest' asilo ameno e grato del reposo il terren") in Gluck's *Orfeo*. It answers to every demand that the definition of felicity can make upon it. It is the music of beings who were once human but are now above and beyond humanity; it has the placid flow of some fabled river of the golden primal time. It is the music of Elysium; and of felicity Elysium is the true home.

LIVING MASTERS OF MUSIC

Edited by ROSA NEWMARCH

An Illustrated Series of Monographs dealing with Contemporary
Musical Life, and including Representatives of
all Branches of the Art

Crown 8vo. Cloth. 3s. 6d. net

Volumes already Published

RICHARD STRAUSS. By ERNEST NEWMAN
HENRY J. WOOD. By ROSA NEWMARCH
SIR EDWARD ELGAR. By R. J. BUCKLEY
JOSEPH JOACHIM. By J. A. FULLER MAITLAND
THEODOR LESCHETIZKY. By ANNETTE HULLAH
GIACOMO PUCCINI. By WAKELING DRY
ALFRED BRUNEAU. By ARTHUR HERVEY
IGNAZ PADEREWSKI. By E. A. BAUGHAN
CLAUDE DEBUSSY. By Mrs FRANZ LIEBICH
GRANVILLE BANTOCK. By H. ORSMOND ANDERTON

THE MUSIC OF THE MASTERS

Edited by WAKELING DRY

Foolscap 8vo. With Portrait. 2s. 6d. net each vol.

ELGAR. By ERNEST NEWMAN
WAGNER. By ERNEST NEWMAN
BRAHMS. By H. C. COLLES
BACH. By RUTLAND BOUGHTON
TCHAIKOVSKI. By E. MARKHAM LEE, M.A., Mus. Doc.
BEETHOVEN. By ERNEST WALKER, M.A., D.Mus.
(Oxon.)

JOHN LANE, THE BODLEY HEAD, VIGO ST., W.1

Lightning Source UK Ltd.
Milton Keynes UK
UKHW022113080223
416681UK00011B/2627